1ST

D0295981

THE NORTH BERWICK STORY

THE
NORTH BERWICK
STORY

Rev. Walter M. Ferrier, M.A., B.D.
Minister at North Berwick; Parish Church of St Andrew

ROYAL BURGH OF NORTH BERWICK COMMUNITY COUNCIL
1980

First published November 1980
by the Royal Burgh of North Berwick Community Council
Atholl Lodge, 13 East Road, North Berwick
East Lothian, Scotland, EH39 4LF

© Walter M. Ferrier
all rights reserved

Printed in Great Britain by Lindsay & Co. Ltd.,
16 Orwell Terrace, Edinburgh

Coat of Arms of the Royal Burgh of North Berwick

FOREWORD

NOW, AFTER many years of hope and anticipation, we have an authoritative history of North Berwick. For this we are greatly indebted to the Rev. Walter Ferrier. He has produced for us not only a work of scholarship and learning, but one so readable and full of interest that it is easy for those of us who now live in the Royal Burgh to relate effortlessly to our predecessors of earlier times.

Those who truly love North Berwick, and they are many, will find in this book a fascinating chronicle about our forebears — who they were and what they did; their way of life and their traditions; their successes and their failures. I also hope they will find in it an inspiration to continue to work for the preservation of the Royal Burgh as a happy and prosperous place to live in, with a thriving community which is ready to grasp the best the future has to offer whilst at the same time respecting the achievements and values of the past.

Walter Ferrier, the author of the book, and the Community Council, who so wisely commissioned it, should be immensely proud of the North Berwick Story.

Leuchie,
North Berwick.

ABOUT THIS BOOK

THIS IS an attempt at a history of North Berwick, written for everybody, whether new to North Berwick or native. It is written in the hope that it contains something of interest to all.

When the Community Council of North Berwick invited me to write a book about North Berwick and its past, my first thought was that the one man who could have done this to perfection, Dr J. S. Richardson, LL.D., H.R.S.A., F.R.I.A.S., F.S.A.(Scot.), formerly Inspector of Ancient Monuments for Scotland, had unfortunately died some years ago without having done so. Brought up in North Berwick, he knew it thoroughly, and lost no opportunity, particularly during his retirement in North Berwick, to probe farther into its history. His interest in the burgh's activities was strong, very personal, and continued over a very long period. As long ago as 1905, James Richardson was drawing humorous cartoons of the Provost and various members of the Town Council of the day. Something of his enthusiasm for history must have rubbed off on me, for my second thought about the Community Council's invitation was that I should accept without too much demur. Now that the book has been written, I gladly acknowledge that without Dr Richardson's inspiration and insight, this would be a much worse book than it is. My debt to him will be obvious on page after page.

Each person writes history in his own way, from his own standpoint, because the writing of history is not an exact science but a form of art, involving, as all art does, selection of material and interpretation of material, both of which reflect the personal characteristics of the writer. Readers will have no difficulty in seeing the mind of a minister of the Church at work in this book — yet perhaps it is not purely personal bias which is responsible for the "ecclesiastical" flavour of the first two chapters. There are in fact only a few non-ecclesiastical sources for this period, and even the ecclesiastical sources are used with the intention of illuminating the life-style of the period. If this book has the effect of provoking another historian to write another history of

North Berwick from another viewpoint, this can only be pure gain.

At all events, I thank the Community Council for their stimulus to me to write, and can only express the hope that this book realises at least some of their hopes, and only a few of their fears.

WALTER M. FERRIER,
Manse of St Andrew,
North Berwick.

October 1980.

CONTENTS

Earliest Times   1

The Middle Ages   12

North Berwick in the later Middle Ages   23

Times of the Reformation   33

Speak of the Devil   38

The Seventeenth Century   44

The Eighteenth Century — and later   56

"The Biarritz of the North"   66

Recent Times, 1914-1939   81

Sources and Authorities   88

Acknowledgments   93

Index   94

LIST OF ILLUSTRATIONS

	facing page
Coat of Arms of the Royal Burgh	i
East Bay, 1836	2
Bass Rock before 1902	6
Baldred's Territory from Soutra	7
North Berwick about 1830	
Seal of the Nunnery (late twelfth century)	
Seal of the Nunnery (fifteenth century)	12/13
Tiles made at North Berwick Nunnery	
Mould for Pilgrims' badges	13
The "Cat's Close"	16
The ruins of "The Newark", 1880's	17
"Doctor Fian" and friend	42
Ruins on Bass Rock (before 1902)	46
Ruins of fortress on Bass Rock (before 1902)	47
North Berwick Parish Church (1664-1883)	50
Inside North Berwick Parish Church	51
"Goodall's Corner" about 1900	52
Appeal for funds to build a Free Church	53
North Berwick Pipe Band, 1901	58
Quality Street in the 1880's	59
The lifeboat *Fergus Ferguson*	64
Launching of the *Fergus Ferguson*	66
Queen Victoria Diamond Jubilee Procession	67
A topsail schooner in the harbour	68
Dirleton Avenue before 1888	69
In the gasworks (Station Hill)	70
Post Office and staff about 1903	71
Ben Sayers, 1857-1924	72
View from the Platcock Rocks	73

	facing page
Invitation to Royal Arrival at Station	74
Train at North Berwick Station (1920's)	75
The Prince and Princess of Saxe-Weimar	76
King Edward VII planting a tree	77
Paddle steamer *Redgauntlet*	78
Paddle steamer *Tantallon Castle*	79
Charabanc of the 1920's	82
"The Pierrots", 1924	83
Site of modern housing development	84
"The Gunboat"	85

The East Bay, 1836

EARLIEST TIMES

THE BEGINNING of the North Berwick Story, like the story of every other locality, may be said to be shrouded in the proverbial mists of antiquity. The long aeons stretching back to Man's first appearance on these shores are anonymous and shadowy. Up to the moment of writing, there have been known in North Berwick only two places where the work of early man may be seen. The first of these is the area on the south side of the Law, above the quarry where, in the soil, traces of an early kitchen midden have been detected. The second is the structure known as Castle Hill, the tumulus projecting northwards from the high ground overlooking the houses in Marine Parade, and dividing them from those in Tantallon Terrace.

These, however, can hardly be considered historical sources, and we must therefore leave them to the science of archaeology to investigate and interpret.

The first appearance of names on the historical scene comes from the period of the Roman occupation of what is now Lowland Scotland. Intermittently throughout the first few centuries of our era the Roman legions came and went, as the fortunes of war dictated the frontier between the Pax Romana and the warlike tribes to the north. Sometimes the frontier would be Hadrian's Wall between Solway and Tyne — sometimes the Antonine Wall between Bowling and Kinneil. At other times, Roman camps in Perthshire and farther north would be occupied. Their policy towards the native tribes within the Wall was straightforward — so long as they served, and did not interfere with, the purposes of military occupation, a relationship of trade and mutual cooperation might grow and flourish. But if there were any resistance to Rome, the force of the legions might be used to bring them to a proper state of respect and obedience. The tribe mentioned in Roman literature as living in what is now south-east Scotland was the Votadini (sometimes the form Otadeni is found). They would appear to have been a peaceful and cooperative people, as there are no remains of any military works in the area, apart from that at

1

Inveresk, which served general military purposes. North Berwick has no Roman ruin, nor is there any other known in East Lothian. The Votadini, like other tribes in Britain identified by the Romans, would speak a language belonging to the Brythonic group (i.e., a Celtic language of that sub-family of which Welsh, Cornish and Breton are members). There is evidence that such a language was spoken in East Lothian in post-Roman times. Legend also speaks of a fortified settlement on top of Traprain Law in that era, belonging to a tribe of Romanised Britons. Perhaps their greatest legacy to the present day is a group of place-names in East Lothian which can be traced to a language of a Brythonic type. The following are examples:

Present form of name	Older name	Possible Brythonic original	Meaning
Tantallon	Dentaloun	Dyn talgwn	"Towering fortress"
	Dunpelder (Traprain Law)	Dyn Pelydyr	"fortress of staves" (i.e., wooden palisade)
Yester		Ystre	"house"
Peffer (stream)		Pefr	"sparkling"
?Aberlady	Aberlessic	Aber llesg	"sluggish river-mouth"

With the coming of the Anglo-Saxons, the Brythonic-speaking tribes were pushed westwards, to appear as the Britons of Strathclyde, while in the east the kingdom of Northumbria was being established.

The name North Berwick has had several suggested derivations. In the author's view, the most likely derivation is from the Old English. Barley is a crop which has been raised in East Lothian from the earliest times, traces of this grain having been found at the kitchen-midden site already mentioned; and Bere is the Old English word for barley. We still use this word, applying it now to the fermented liquor of sprouting barley. Bere, then, might supply the first syllable of the word Berwick. The second syllable, Wic, means dwelling or village in Old

English. So Berwick would mean the barley village. The word North would be applied to distinguish this Berwick from Berwick-upon-Tweed, which throughout part of the Middle Ages was not an English but a Scottish city, and was then known to the Scots as South Berwick. It is still permissible, however, to omit the word North when speaking of our local hill as Berwick Law. Two hundred years ago Robert Burns referred to it in these terms in his poem "Gae bring to me a pint o' wine". Until recently, the name of one of the boats of the Forth Pilotage Authority which used North Berwick harbour was *Berwick Law*.

In the state of Maine, U.S.A., there is another North Berwick which, at the time of writing, is celebrating the 150th anniversary of its foundation. It is unlikely, however, that there is any direct connection between it and the North Berwick of this book. As many of the town-names in the state of Maine derive from their counterparts in the south of England, it is more likely that North Berwick, Maine, along with its neighbours Berwick and South Berwick, Maine, take their names from a Berwick either in Sussex or in Hampshire. The Berwick in Sussex is mentioned as Berewice in Domesday Book (c. 1087 A.D.).

By the eighth century, there emerges the name of Baldred, a pioneer Christian Missionary and leader of life in East Lothian at that early time. His name is familiar to all in North Berwick, through St Baldred's Episcopal Church in Dirleton Avenue, St Baldred's Road, St Baldred's Crescent, St Baldred's Tower, a large red stone building overlooking the tennis courts, St Baldred's Chapel on the Bass Rock, and the church of Prestonkirk (East Linton) which is a St Baldred dedication. Those who knew North Berwick in earlier years will remember the pleasure launch *St Baldred* which took visitors to Fidra and round the Bass.

While the connection between Baldred and North Berwick is not explicit in history, the town contains so many uses of his name that some account of him is necessary in a history of North Berwick.

At a range of 1,200 years, it is not easy for the twentieth century investigator to lay down a reliable factual history of such a man, especially when it is remembered that about 400 years elapsed between his life and the earliest known written material about him. This earliest material is in itself extremely sparse, and comes from the pen of Symeon, a monk of Durham, who

3

died in 1133. Much later, nearer the time of the Reformation, there was published the *Aberdeen Breviary*. This book contains biographical notes on many "local" Scottish saints, and includes St Baldred. Of him, it states that he died in the year 606 A.D., that he was a disciple of St Kentigern (who was also known as St Mungo, patron saint of Glasgow), and that he founded churches at Tyninghame, Auldhame and Preston (meaning Prestonkirk, East Linton). The first two of these statements are, to say the least, questionable. They place Baldred 150 years earlier than Symeon does, and can be understood only in the light of the late mediaeval Scottish church's desire to present history in such a way that no English archbishop could make a claim to a prior "conquest" of Scottish territory by a missionary from south of what was then the border.

To return to Symeon, however — though he was a voluminous writer, there are only three sentences in all his writings in which Baldred is mentioned. So the task of the historian becomes one of extracting the maximum possible information from the meagre evidence. It may be of interest to quote Symeon's exact words:

(1) Speaking of Bishop Friothubert of Hexham, Symeon says:

Huius pontificatus anno xvii, regni vero Eadberti vicesimo, vir Domini et Presbyter Baltherus, qui vitam anachoreticam in Tiningaham duxerat, viam sanctorum patrum ingressus est, migrando ad eum qui se reformavit ad imaginem Filii sui pridie nonas Martias.

(Translation — On the day before the Nones of March (i.e., 6th March) in the seventeenth year of the episcopate of this bishop, and in the twentieth year of the reign of Eadbert, that man of the Lord, the priest Balthere, who had been living the life of a recluse at Tiningaham, entered upon the path of the holy fathers and departed to Him who had created him anew, even to the image of His Son.)

This places the death of Baldred on 6th March in the year 757 A.D.

(2) Telling the life story of Cuthbert, Symeon is describing how Cuthbert was appointed Bishop of Lindisfarne. He then goes on to describe the boundaries of the diocese of Lindisfarne, by reference to various rivers in what is

4

now Northumberland, and also north of the Cheviots. He then adds that the diocese included:

tota terra quae pertinet ad monasterium Sancti Balthere quod vocatur Tiningaham, a Lombormore usque ad Escemuthe.

(Translation — . . . all the land which belongs to the monastery of Saint Balthere which is called Tiningaham, from Lombormore to Escemuthe.)

(3) Copying possibly from an earlier chronicle, Symeon records:

Anno DCCCCXLI — Olilaf, vastata ecclesia Sancti Balteri et incensa Tiningaham, mox periit.

(Translation — In the year 941 — Olilaf, having devasted the church of Saint Balthere and having burnt Tiningaham, shortly died.)

These extracts introduce us to East Lothian, and particularly to Tyninghame, as they were in an age long before the division of our island into an England in the south and a Scotland in the north. This was the age of the small independent kingdoms. Baldred's country was Northumbria, a kingdom which stretched from the Humber to the Forth, and his language would be Anglo-Saxon. The official religion, upheld by royal authority, was Christianity. This had been brought to Northumbria 200 years or so previously by Aidan, a monk of Iona. Following the example of his respected Abbot Columba, Aidan had chosen an island, Lindisfarne or Holy Island, as a base for his mission. In passing, it may be of interest to note that in the course of time this was a particularly successful mission, for as a result of it, much of what is now England north of the Thames was evangelised, anticipating Augustine's arrival in Kent.

Northumbria, by Baldred's time, could boast its men of learning. The Venerable Bede, monk of Jarrow and outstanding historian of the Anglo-Saxon period, died only 25 years or so before the death of Baldred. Then there had been Wilfrid, Bishop of Hexham, who had led the Romanising party at the Synod of Whitby in 664 A.D. He had travelled widely, and had even, as his biographer Eddius Stephanus tells, suffered imprisonment at Dunbar! From his journey to Rome, Wilfrid is said to have brought back to Hexham the reputed relics of the Apostle Andrew. In the lowlands north of the Cheviots, a princess of the royal line, Aebba, had instituted a monastery at

Coldingham, and another had been planted at Old Melrose at a place, as Bede tells, where the winding Tweed almost completely encircled the ground in a great loop. Best known south of the Forth, however, was Cuthbert, the hill shepherd turned monk-evangelist, whose name is remembered in church dedications in Edinburgh, in Kirkcudbright, and in many other places. Following Symeon's dating of Baldred's death in 757 A.D., Baldred would live and work about 30 or 40 years after Cuthbert. This chronology has supporting evidence from local archaeology. Three stone cross shafts, independently attributable to the eighth or ninth century, have been found, one at Tyninghame, one at Morham, and the third at Aberlady. These may be taken as confirming the activity of an eighth century Saxon mission in these localities.

The second of Symeon's references to Baldred contains the information that there was a monastery at Tyninghame, owing its existence to Baldred and bearing his name. His earlier reference had called Baldred a recluse, but here it is implied that he is a leader of a monastic community. Historians have tended to think of Baldred as a solitary figure, living a hermit's life on the Bass Rock and occasionally crossing to the mainland on tours of preaching and teaching. While doubtless an eighth century monk might use the Bass as a place of retreat for prayer and meditation during Lent, say, or at other times, it is unlikely that Baldred would be purely a hermit. With the responsibilities of a monastery, the supervision of its activities which would include agriculture, forestry, stone-masonry, and the production of beautiful copies of Biblical and devotional literature in its scriptorium, Baldred's would be a busy life lived out in the company of others. Such monasteries were known to contain about 200 monks, many of them engaged in the specialised occupations mentioned above.

A further feature of interest in the second of Symeon's references is the description of the territory attributed to Baldred's monastery at Tyninghame — "a Lombormore usque ad Escemuthe" "Lombormore" is the earlier form of the word Lammermuir, and means "the lambs' moor" — i.e., the moorland pasture on which lambs were fattened. "Escemuthe" is an Anglo-Saxon form of a word which is more familiar to us in its Gaelic translation as Inveresk — the mouth or confluence of the River Esk. So Baldred's territory stretched from the

The Bass Rock before 1902 showing St Baldred's Chapel, above the ruins of the fortress

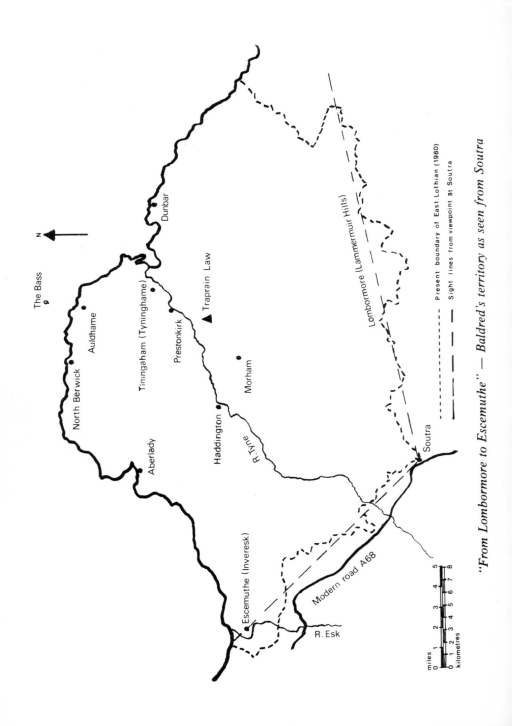

"From Lombormore to Escemuthe" — Baldred's territory as seen from Soutra

The Bass

N

Dunbar

Auldhame

Traprain Law

Tiningham (Tyninghame)

North Berwick

Prestonkirk

Morham

Aberlady

Haddington

R. Tyne

Escemuthe (Inveresk)

Modern road A68

R. Esk

Lombormore (Lammermuir Hills)

Soutra

———— Present boundary of East Lothian (1980)

·········· Sight lines from viewpoint at Soutra

miles
0   1   2   3   4   5
0 1 2 3 4 5 6 7 8
kilometres

Lammermuir Hills to Inveresk. This always seemed to the author to be a very unsatisfactory description of an area, and one which would never occur to anyone normally living on the Lothian plain. Then, one day, returning northwards from the direction of Jedburgh along the present A68 road, the author was presented with a solution. As one looks northwards from the top of Soutra Hill, one has a magnificent panoramic view of the Lothian plain. Indeed, the word Soutra is said to derive from the Brythonic *Sol Tref*, meaning "outlook house". If an observer, standing in this position extends his right arm he marks the line of the Lammermuir Hills. He may then bring his arm round to point in a roughly north-westerly direction, aiming at Inveresk. In carrying out this movement of the arm, the observer has swept out an area of land whose boundaries are found to be roughly coincident with the boundaries of East Lothian, or of the Deanery of Lothian of the church of the Middle Ages. Symeon's description is seen to be a vectorial one, and the turning centre of the vector is Soutra. The description he gives is such as would occur naturally to an observer who has travelled from south of the Lammermuirs, roughly along the line of the present A68, has halted at the top of Soutra Hill, and has delineated the land spread out before him by the method described above. It may not be too far-fetched to conceive that in using the words "a Lombormore usque ad Escemuthe" Symeon was copying a description due originally to Baldred himself as he surveyed the land which was to be the scene of his life's work. If this is the case, it is to Baldred in the first place that the boundaries of East Lothian are due. There is also the further consequence that if Baldred's view of his territory is that of one seeing it from the top of Soutra Hill, it must be from south of Soutra that Baldred came in the first place. In which case, the conclusion is well-nigh irresistible that Baldred was sent out as a missionary, along with his "family" of monks, from the monastery of Old Melrose, to which reference has already been made, some 19 miles to the south. In Baldred's time, there would be still some remains of the Roman road, the northward extension of Dere Street, from Newstead (Trimontium) to Inveresk. At Inveresk there had been a Roman fort with, some say, a temple to Jupiter on the spot now occupied by St Michael's Church. Later, in the sixth century, St Modwenna is said to have founded a Christian church there. At all events, whatever building occupied that site, it would be a well-known landmark, even in Baldred's day. At the southern end of the road, Old Melrose is only a short distance from Newstead.

The date of Baldred's arrival in East Lothian can only be roughly guessed at. Starting with the death of Baldred in 757 and allowing a period of 30 or 40 years for his life's work, we arrive at a date somewhere between 717 and 727 A.D. The author is indebted to the late Dr J. S. Richardson for the idea that Bede's Church History contains a story in which there is the possibility (to put it no higher) that there is a clue to this problem. Briefly, Bede's story is of a man of evil habits who lived at a place he calls, in Latin, Incuneningum, who died and whose soul was escorted by an angel, first, to view Purgatory, then the mouth of Hell itself. Pleading with the angel for another chance in life, he was at length permitted to return to earth, and was welcomed by his amazed and weeping relations, but from this time on, his life was changed. He became a monk and entered the monastery of Old Melrose, gladly accepting its ascetic disciplines and its mortifications of the flesh. Dr Richardson's theory was that the word Incuneningum may be interpreted as a copyists's error for Intiningaham, which would be Bede's way of saying "At Tyninghame" in Latin, and that this was a possible reference to the work of a Christian mission, and Christian teaching, at Tyninghame, which was backed up by the monastic community at Old Melrose. The case can be extended farther by the application of dating. Bede states clearly that he had this story on the highest and best authority, and that it all happened "while Aethelwald was Abbot of Old Melrose". According to Florence of Worcester, Aethelwald left Old Melrose to become Bishop of Lindisfarne in the year 721. So perhaps Baldred had arrived and was at work prior to that year. But the evidence is admittedly very thin.

As for the extent of Baldred's work, the three places mentioned in the *Aberdeen Breviary,* Tyninghame, Auldhame and Prestonkirk, lie within a circle of only 4¼ miles diameter, but the cross shafts from Morham and Aberlady already mentioned, indicate a wider coverage for Baldred's mission. North Berwick, such as it may have been in that early age, would be familiar with Baldred's monks, and with Baldred himself. But North Berwick may have seen another early Christian pioneer, under somewhat different circumstances.

Mention has been made of Wilfrid, Bishop of Hexham, and his bringing of the reputed relics of St Andrew to Hexham. When he died in 709, his successor in office, Acca, inherited his famous collection of books and relics. But, as the continuator of Bede's History records, in 731, he was expelled from his see. Five years later, the "Chronicles of the Picts and the Scots" records that the St Andrew relics were now in Fife, at the town which bears the Apostle's name. From that time on, the patron saint of the Pictish kingdom, and later of the Scottish kingdom, was St Andrew. If it is accepted that Acca travelled from Hexham to St Andrews bearing the holy relics; and if it is accepted that he travelled over land to the south coast of the Forth estuary, this might explain the dedications to St Andrew in these localities. The parish church of St Andrew, North Berwick is one. It must be an early dedication, as it is not among the list of dedications performed by Bishop David de Bernham in 1242, and was already known as a St Andrew church by 1177. Then there is the St Andrew's Well in the Lodge grounds, within the "Wall Tower"; there is the parish church of Gullane, and there was a St Andrew's well on the Isle of May. These dedications may well have been performed by Acca in virtue of the "personal presence" of the saint, as represented by his relics. This not to say, however, that there was no place of worship at the site of the old church of North Berwick until Acca's time. Acca might choose to dedicate an already existing site in the name of the Apostle.

To return to Baldred, there has been discussion in scholastic circles on whether Baldred, in addition to setting up places of Christian worship and burial, may have contributed material about the early life of St Kentigern which in later ages was included in biographies of the saint. If Baldred was not, as the *Aberdeen Breviary* claims, a disciple and therefore a contemporary of Kentigern, could he not at least have known about Kentigern, and could he not have passed on to posterity, perhaps in written form, information about his ancestry and birth? While such a theory cannot be put to the test for lack of evidence, it stands to reason that a man of letters living and working in East Lothian would be in a favourable position to collect and record tales about Kentigern, which would be nearly 200 years old in Baldred's time. It will be remembered that, according to one version of his biography, Kentigern was the love-begotten offspring of the princess Thenew and a shepherd-boy. Thenew was the daughter of the chieftain King Loth, who ruled the countryside from his fortress on Traprain Law in the sixth century, and whose name is preserved in our word Lothian, which would start life as an adjective, meaning "belonging to King Loth". For her misconduct, Thenew was sentenced to be banished by being cast adrift in an open boat at a place called Aberlessic. Winds and currents drifted the boat towards the Fife shore, and she was rescued by the monks of St Serf from Culross. It was while she was in their care that Kentigern was born. This early part of the Kentigern story must have been recorded by someone with intimate knowledge of East Lothian. Perhaps it was Baldred.

Symeon's third reference takes us to the tenth century, a period when the Danes were active, invading the east coast of our island and sending marauding parties far and wide, round to the west coast, and even establishing permanent settlements as far west as Ireland. While Symeon speaks of a raid by Olilaf, other versions of this chronicle give the name of the leader as Anlaf the Dane, and one version calls him Olaf Godfreyson, King of Dublin. This raid at the mouth of the East Lothian Tyne brought to an end the work of the Baldred monastery at Tyninghame, but there are some who believe that relics of its life are still to be seen in the find of silver from Traprain Law. Just after the First World War, excavation on the west side of Traprain Law revealed a cache of silver, in the form of strips of silver sheet, cut and rolled as if for the melting pot. When suitably treated and fitted like the pieces of a jigsaw puzzle, they made a large number of beautiful plates, bowls and other articles of silver. They were at that time thought to be the proceeds of a pirate raid on shipping; but some have claimed that these were the property of Baldred's monastery, whose site lies only about 5 miles from the point of discovery. One of the articles has a specifically Christian significance. It is a strainer whose perforations take the form of the words IESUS CHRISTUS. Such an article might be of use in the preparation of wine for the Sacrament. Some of this "Treasure of Traprain" may be seen in the Scottish National Museum of Antiquities in Edinburgh.

In the age that was to follow, the name of Tyninghame was not forgotten. The church of the Middle Ages had a Dean of

Tyninghame. Even as late as the eve of the Reformation, one of the titles of the Archbishop of St Andrews was Lord Tyninghame. The memory of Baldred himself was honoured by two miracle-tales, one which tells of a rock which was a danger to shipping, lying between the Bass and the mainland, which, at the word of the holy man, floated away to the shore. This became known as "Baldred's Boat". The second tale is about the death of Baldred. According to this legend, when Baldred died, a dispute arose among the three churches he had founded, Tyninghame, Auldhame and Prestonkirk, which of the three should have the honour of possessing his body. At length, on the advice of a wise man, all three agreed to make it a matter of prayer, and to "sleep on it" overnight. In the morning, three identical bodies of Baldred were found, one in each of the three churches.

Following the destruction of Tyninghame in 941, nothing is known for over 100 years about this area, until a new age had dawned, and a new kind of life-style had been established — that of the Middle Ages.

THE MIDDLE AGES

IT HAS BEEN the custom for historians to take the coronation of the Emperor Charlemagne at Aachen on Christmas Day, 800 A.D. to mark the beginning of the Middle Ages in Europe. This era saw at its zenith a society based on a Feudal System which in its turn was based on the tenure of land and property. Its second feature was a Christian Church, richly endowed with land and property by the munificence of kings and nobles, gifted with men of high intelligence, strongly organised locally in parishes, with an intermediate executive arm consisting of bishops, archbishops and other officials and with an authoritarian centre at Rome in the person of the Bishop of Rome, the Pope. By common consent he was acknowledged as earthly head of this vast international omnipresence, and hailed as Vicar of Christ.

Scotland, however, situated on the north-west fringe of the European scene, did not enter the Middle Ages proper until much later than the continent. It was not in fact until the coming of Queen Margaret who married King Malcolm III (Canmore) of Scots in 1070 that the process of mediaevalisation got under way. But in the meantime several important changes had been taking place in the previous century or so since the year 941. The two Celtic Kingdoms, of the Picts and of the Scots, had already been united in the late eighth century under King Kenneth MacAlpin, whose kingdom now therefore stretched from the far north to the Forth estuary. Later, Lothian was added by conquest to the territory of the King of Scots. Consequently the Gaelic language was now heard in East Lothian. Several landmarks in the locality of North Berwick bear witness to this in the derivation of their names. Words like Craigleith and Leithies come from this period, while on the farm of Newhouse there is a field called Kilmurdie. This name clearly has Gaelic derivation, and can only mean "the cell of Murdo", i.e. a little building used as a place of prayer by a man called Murdo, who might be a hermit or holy man dating from this time.

Seen through the eyes of her biographer, Turgot, Queen

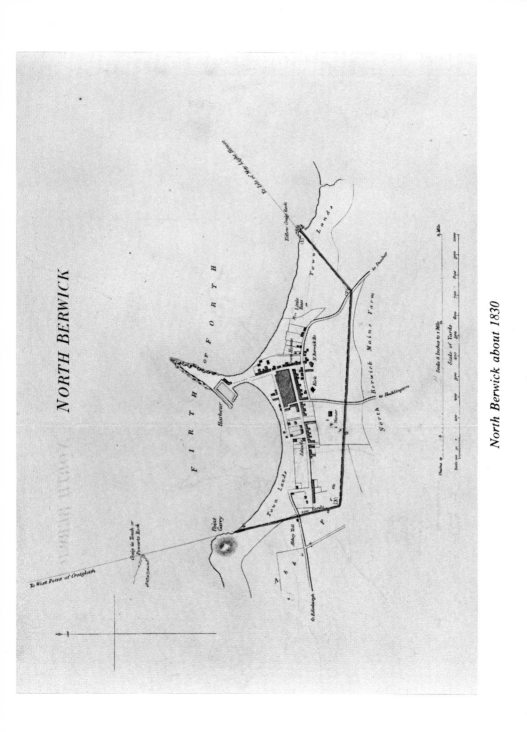

North Berwick about 1830

Seal of the Nunnery
late 12th century

Seal of the Nunnery
15th century

Tiles made at North Berwick Nunnery

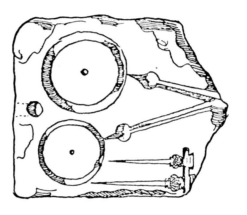

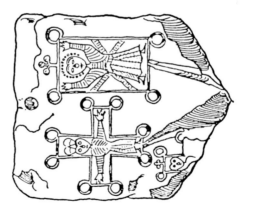

Mould for casting pilgrims' badges, found at the church near the harbour

Margaret was a woman of great piety and charity. She was also a woman of indomitable purpose. She made it her business, among other things, to bring the Christian Church as she found it in her new kingdom into more direct relation with the Rome-oriented church of the remainder of Western Europe as she had known it in earlier life.

Our interest in her arises from her encouragement of pilgrimages to St Andrew's in Fife. There, the reputed relics of the first disciple lay enshrined. These were said to consist of an arm-bone and several finger-bones, and they would be displayed, not as in a show-case in a museum, for the curious to gaze at, but in a precious and purpose-made reliquary, possibly of gold and crystal. It has been suggested that this might take the form of a hollow human forearm and hand, mounted vertically, with the thumb and first and second fingers extended in a posture of blessing, and with the bones visible through a crystal "window" in the arm and hand. People would come in their thousands from vast distances to worship and pray in the presence of the holy relics. Holidays, as we understand them, might be unknown, but pilgrimages to holy places like St Andrews were always popular. The Forth estuary, however, was a barrier to travellers from the south. Margaret therefore set up a ferry at the shortest crossing of the Forth, at Queensferry. In modern days this is now spanned by the Forth railway bridge, and the newer suspension road bridge. The names of North and South Queensferry, of course, originate from this royally instituted ferry. As a further help to pilgrims coming from the direction of Berwick-on-Tweed, north-east England or the borders, a ferry was started between North Berwick on the south side of the Forth, and Earlsferry on the north. The Earls of Fife were at this time great land-owners not only in Fife, but also in the North Berwick area. Till the time of King Robert II they held the barony of North Berwick "with the castle" — i.e., with Tantallon. Then in 1371 these lands south of the Forth passed into the hands of William, first Earl of Douglas. To serve the needs of pilgrims using this ferry, hospices were built, one on each side of the water, and there was a church at Earlsferry, a small stone building on a knoll overlooking the harbour. On the south shore, North Berwick had its hospice, and its church also, close to the harbour. This church was a much larger building than the present outlines indicate, and it may have been built on the site of a previous building. As for the hospice at North Berwick, it is likely to have stood close to the church and the harbour. In a drawing of North Berwick dating from the eighteenth century, the work of Colonel Hutton, now in the National Library of Scotland, there can be seen just to the north-west of the old church three blocks of masonry, which, in the opinion of the late Dr J. S. Richardson, may have been the last remains of the hospice.

At its busiest period, it is said that the ferry carried as many as ten thousand pilgrims a year. This pilgrim traffic must have been an outstanding feature of life in the little town of North Berwick in the Middle Ages — for North Berwick would indeed be a tiny place then, for as late as the eighteenth century, the population of the town was only about 700, and it cannot have been greater in the Middle Ages. Little wonder, then, that when in 1373 North Berwick was granted its charter as a Royal Burgh by King Robert II, it should be the ferry-boat that was chosen as the theme of its heraldic bearings. These depict a small boat with four oarsmen each wearing a Scots bonnet, a mast and a furled sail, the lion at the prow, the cross of St Andrew at the masthead, and a crowned figure dressed in ermine at the stern. It is possible that this is a representation of the Earl of Douglas, while the cross of St Andrew emphasises the pilgrim theme.

While it is possible that the ferry boat would leave from some point very near the church — the location of the present harbour might be a likely place — yet there is evidence connecting the ferry with the Broad Sands, which lie to the west of the Eil burn in the parish of Dirleton. On such a broad and flat strand the ferry boat could easily be beached. Further, the shortest crossing of the Forth estuary at this part is from the Broad Sands to Earlsferry — a distance of $8\frac{1}{4}$ miles. It is also significant that there is near at hand the farm called Ferrygate (meaning "the road to the ferry").

Shortly after the First World War, a stone mould for casting pilgrims' badges was unearthed from the site of the old parish church at the harbour. This is now in North Berwick Museum. Among the emblems this mould could produce is the figure of St Andrew on his diagonal cross, with loops whereby the badge can be sewn on to the pilgrim's hat, as a token that he had visited this (St Andrew's) church, and had undertaken the pilgrimage to St Andrews in Fife.

In addition to the pilgrims, the North Berwick ferry had some distinguished passengers. In 1303 John Deugaigne, valet de chambre to the Prince of Wales (later, King Edward II of England) crossed the firth on the way to Dunfermline with £400 brought from London for the King of England's household. The following year, 2,000 merks intended for King Edward himself at Dunfermline were carried over by the North Berwick ferry.

Pilgrims continued to pass through North Berwick throughout the Middle Ages, but as the centuries wore on, the pilgrim traffic declined until by the sixteenth century it had become a mere trickle. This decline coincides with the decline in public belief in pilgrimages, especially at times when the pressures of Renaissance and Reformation were at work throughout Europe. One traveller, James Melville, Professor of Hebrew at St Andrews, writing in September 1586, stated that the boat on which he crossed the Forth was old and dirty, having been used for carrying coal, and the one man who ferried him was old also. By 1692 North Berwick had no ferryboats.

Besides founding the ferry successive holders of the Earldom of Fife were responsible for giving and confirming gifts of lands, churches and other endowments, to a nunnery in North Berwick, founded by the then Earl of Fife some time before 1154. This nunnery was originally a Benedictine house, though in later centuries it is referred to as being of the Cistertian Order. It was ruled over by a Prioress, so it is sometimes correctly referred to as a Priory. Yet, strangely, in 1297, the name is found of one "James, Prior of North Berwick".

While nothing whatsoever remains of the nunnery buildings at the present time, there can be no doubt that their site was that of the present Abbey Old People's Home. This is a nineteenth century house, formerly the property of the Speir family, and known as "the Abbey". In the ancient charters, the name of the land on which the Abbey was built is given as Gillecalmestun. There is, in Old Abbey Road, a ruined building which some may refer to as "the Abbey" but this is not correct. This ruin is of a private house, built in the sixteenth century of the stone of the original Abbey, belonging to Alexander Home, "the Gudeman of North Berwick", about whom more will be said in a later chapter.

In the garden of the present Old People's Home human bones have been unearthed from time to time, indicative of a conventual graveyard. The nunnery also had a well which is in the garden of a house named Oldfields (so named by its builder, the late Capt. John Wallace, because it was on the old fields of the Abbey). To provide for winter feeding, the nunnery had a dovecote to the south-east of the conventual buildings, which, it is estimated, could contain 1,320 pigeons. At the heart of the nunnery's life there would be the church, which was dedicated to St Mary by Bishop David de Bernham on 10th October 1242. One of the consecration crosses of that church was discovered when some buildings of the former Abbey Farm were being dismantled in preparation for the construction of the present telephone exchange.

One special feature of the site is that there were four tile kilns. Remains of these are to be seen in an etching of 1789, which also shows the dovecote. It is likely that they were situated on the low ground on the south-east of the site.

While the nature of a nun's calling implies disengagement from the world and its affairs, it was otherwise with the nunnery as a whole which, because of its endowments of land, had extensive relations of trade and agriculture with the outside world. The following are some notes on the special activities of the nunnery of North Berwick.

(a) *Agriculture*

The land immediately surrounding the Abbey would be well provided with seaweed, which was extensively used, possibly along with lime, as a fertiliser in the Middle Ages. This is evident from the fact that at least two roads are still traceable leading up from the beach to the abbey precincts. One is called Ware Road to this day, and ware means seaweed. This Ware Road starts on the sands to the west of Point Garry as a cart-track crossing the golf course and passing between the house called Winterfield and the houses in Cromwell Road. It continues then as a pathway leading to Dirleton Avenue, crossing it and leading to the Abbey as the present Ware Road. A second cart track doubtless used for the same purpose starts from the West Bay and cuts across the links towards the curve on Beach Road. From that point, the way would be clear in earlier centuries for this track to join up with the nungate ("the nuns' road").

(b) *Manufacture of tiles*

The tiles produced in the kilns at the Abbey were of a dark

The "Cats' Close" as it was at the end of last century

The ruins of "the Newark" as they were in the 1880's

brown colour, with a greenish sheen. There are samples in North Berwick Museum. They are mainly square, and carry various designs. A hunting dog is one motif, and the fleur-de-lys another. These tiles would be of use in paving the floors of churches or other buildings, or tiling their walls.

(c) *Milling grain*

To the east of the farthest houses in Tantallon Terrace, the Glen Burn reaches the sea. Before it does so, it passes down through the Glen (also known as the Ladies' Walk). In its path there are three small buildings, now ruinous. These are the Mills of Kintreath, and they were built in the Middle Ages. They were the property of the nunnery, which was entitled to a multure (a percentage of all grain milled). The water-wheels and other mechanisms have of course long since vanished. The Glen Burn, having powered these mills, then went out into the Mill Sea (Hence the name Milsey Bay).

(d) *Wool production*

Wool from the sheep of North Berwick Abbey was known in Italy in the 13th century. Clearly the North Berwick wool had more than a local reputation. Wool was one of the staple exports of North Berwick in the mediaeval period.

Only a few names of North Berwick Prioresses occur in historical documents. Among these are Beatrice (1375), Elena de Carrick (1389), Matilda de Leys (1434) and Margaret Home, the last Prioress before the Reformation, whose signature is visible on a document of 1578. For the most part, however, neither prioresses nor nuns could write. Their calling did not require them to be literate, but only to pray and to take part in the perpetual praise, the *laus sempiterna,* of the Christian Church. When a signature was required, they would simply lay their hand on the pen, as the notary wrote their name for them. But though unable to write, the Prioresses generally were connected with influential families. In the case of Dame Elena de Carrick, for example, we can infer a connection with the Royal Family of Scotland when it is recalled that Robert the Bruce was Earl of Carrick (i.e., de Carrick) before he became King of Scots, and that it was through the marriage of his daughter Marjorie Bruce to Walter the High Steward that the Stuart dynasty took its origin.

For an account of the appearance and personality of a Prioress of those days, the author finds it difficult to avoid

C

thinking of the delightful and gently humorous character-sketch of a prioress given by Geoffrey Chaucer in his Prologue to the Canterbury Tales. This lady, he tells, was charming in every possible way, and very accomplished, especially in those affairs of the world, which, by the rules of her Order, she had no business doing! While this refers to an English Prioress of the 14th century, a Scottish Prioress might not differ greatly. The only reservation might be that a Prioress of an earlier century e.g., the twelfth, would adhere more strictly to the rigorous rules of her Order!

On term-days (Whitsunday and Martinmas) the Prioress would sit at the gate of the nunnery collecting her rents from the tenants on Abbey land.

In addition to the land and the property which it possessed in North Berwick the nunnery was also endowed with other very considerable assets. These were the churches of Maybole (Ayrshire), Logie (near Stirling), Largo (Fife), Kilconquhar (Fife), and North Berwick. These churches themselves had considerable endowments of land, and of rights to tiends (tithes or tenths) of many enterprises — e.g., the produce of farms, most in grain, some in livestock, fishings in rivers and in the Forth, and such like. All these endowments were, in the first place, gifts either from the Earls of Fife or from the Earls of Carrick. The net result was that, like many other religious houses, the North Berwick nunnery was a wealthy establishment, and its assets and revenues were very considerable.

While the affairs of the nunnery went on from day to day, this had little or no bearing on the spiritual needs of the people of the parish of North Berwick. It was not the nunnery, but the parish church, which was meant to bear concern and responsibility for the people generally.

By the generosity of the Earl of Fife, the Prioress and Convent were the owners of the tidal island lying to the north of the town, (the present harbour area) and it was here that the parish church was built some time in the twelfth century. As the church grew in size, a bridging, first of timber, then of stone, was built across the strand, so that eventually the island became a promontory, as at the present day. This island extended a considerable distance eastwards of the present east sea wall, and during the long centuries the sea gradually nibbled away the graveyard to the east of the church, until at length, in the seventeenth century, a violent storm reduced the building to ruins. When first built, the church would be a building of three compartments — nave, choir and presbytery, the latter being the site of the high altar. The building had round-headed doors and windows, and the principal door was on the south side of the nave, near the west end. Directly in line with this door, and within the church stood the baptismal font, on a stepped platform. Later, the church was given a tower at its west end, and then there followed the substitution of arcading on the line of the original side walls of the nave, when the building was widened to give a north and a south aisle. A porch was built on the south side on the axis of the original door and baptismal font. The tower stood some considerable height. On the ground level, it was entered directly from the church. The upper floors gave accommodation for a priest's room, and, above it, a bell chamber. The mediaeval bell which rang there may have been carried away as a trophy of war during a time of turmoil. One of the reasons why the tower remained standing until early last century, and was not quarried away like the rest of the church was that it formed a sea-mark, to give safe navigation to the harbour of North Berwick. It was not until a granary was built to the north of the tower that it was demolished. Since the site of the church was excavated by the late Dr J. S. Richardson in 1951, a collection of early grave stones has been made, most of them now in North Berwick Museum, and the remainder set out in St Ninian's aisle of the church. One of those in the Museum, a little upright slab bearing on both sides an incised cross, is thought to be of about ninth or tenth century date, and may have been a marker to indicate the church's right of sanctuary — i.e., the right — so valuable in a turbulent age — to protect those fleeing from their pursuers, whether wrongdoers or not, till such time as the due process of law could be brought into effect.

Internally, the walls of the church would probably be lime-washed, with coloured patterns in several parts. The floor of the nave might be of clay, but the choir and presbytery would be covered with floor tiles of the kind produced in the kilns of the nunnery. Looking east from the line of the main door, one would see, in the late Middle Ages, the arcading down north and south sides. In the centre one would see the rood screen drawn across the eastern end of the nave. At the top of this screen would be the Rood — i.e., Jesus Christ upon his cross, supported on one side by the Virgin Mary and on the other by St John, "the beloved disciple". The Rood Altar would be placed in close association to this rood screen. The altars in the side aisles would be — in the south aisle, the altar of the Blessed Virgin Mary; it is likely also that St Sebastian's altar would be in this same aisle. The north transept which has been recorded as the Ninian or Carrick Aisle, contained the altar of St Ninian and the Pieta altar, and it was in this aisle that the Douglases, barons of North Berwick, were buried. The High Altar, dedicated to St Andrew, stood at the extreme east end of the church. The graveyard was situated on the east, south and west sides of the church, and it was not until the seventeenth century that the church authorities insisted that all future burials should be on the north side, as interments on the east and south were depriving the ground of the security it should have from storm and tempest.

The first explicit mention of the parish church of St Andrew, North Berwick, occurs in a document of date 1177, in which one of the witnesses is Richard, "Chaplain of Saint Andrew of North Berwick". The author's understanding of this is that here we have the first mention of one who held parish responsibility in North Berwick, and who would regularly celebrate Mass in the parish church.

In 1199 the parish church and the lands of the hospice, along with other endowments, were given to the nunnery by Malcolm, Earl of Fife. The effect of such a gift was that the church building, its endowments of land, the tiends (tithes, or tenths of the produce of the land in question) and the offerings made in church, became the property and responsibility of the nunnery. For its part, the nunnery provided for the maintenance of the services of a priest for the parish church. As he held this office on behalf of the Prioress and nunnery (i.e., vicariously), he now held the title of Vicar of North Berwick. From this time on, it is of Vicars of the parish that documents speak. The Vicar would have for his subsistence a vicarage house and a vicar's croft. The vicarage house, or Manse (Lat. Mansio) stood where the present St Andrew's Church stands, in the High Street, but which at that time would be in open country. Being west of the Clartie Burn (Law Road) the main road at that point would be known as the Westgate. This site was occupied continuously by the Manse over the centuries until 1825 when a new Manse of generous proportions was built on the high ground overlooking the former site.

As for the Vicar's croft or glebe, while a specific statement of its boundaries is not to be found, it cannot have been far from the vicarage house, and it is almost certain to have lain within the area which in 1587 was delineated as the Glebe of North Berwick. These considerations alone point to an area west of Law Road and south of the present St Andrew's Church — the position, in fact, of the traditional North Berwick Glebe. Last century much of that area was used for the building of houses. The boundary of the glebe, as it has been received in modern times, is as follows — starting from the junction of St Andrew Street and Law Road, the boundary goes up Law Road and turns right along Clifford Road. At a point beyond the houses on the right, it turns right, passing to the west of the house called Rosehill (formerly Wonderland), cutting through properties on the south side of Marmion Road, following the stone wall on the north side of Marmion Road which eventually becomes the west wall of No. 19 St Andrew Street. Thence the boundary of the glebe crosses to the north side of St Andrew Street, includes the pavement, and passes east to the starting point.

The vicars were often known by the name of their parish, just as in certain parts farmers are still known to their friends not by their personal surnames, but by the names of their farms. In virtue of their holding of land they could and did take the title ". . . de North Berwick". In 1296, for example, Waldeve, Vicar of North Berwick, has on his seal "S' WALDEVI DE NORBERWIC CL'I" (i.e., Sigillum Waldevi de Norberwic Clerici — The seal of Waldeve of North Berwick, the Cleric or Clerk). Later in the Middle Ages, a priest might also be given the title "Sir" ("Schir" in Scots) though he may not have received the accolade of knighthood. The Sacrament of Ordination to the Priesthood was popularly thought to be like the dubbing of a knight. The ordinand, as it were, becomes God's (or the Pope's) Knight, and therefore entitled to the appellation "Sir".

The first known Vicar of North Berwick was Hugh. His name, alongside those of noble birth, appears as a witness in charters, one dated between 1219 and 1226, and the other 1230. He is "Master Hugh" — that is, he held the degree of

Master of Arts. As there were no universities in Scotland at this time, he must have studied either in England or on the continent. By the year 1242, the Vicar of North Berwick was a man known only by his first initial — J. In this year also, Bishop David de Bernham made his tour in which he dedicated many churches, including the parish church of Gullane and, as already stated, the church of St Mary within the Abbey of North Berwick.

The next known Vicar of North Berwick is David. The only thing known about him is that in 1279 he was arrested at Newcastle-on-Tyne for burglary of the house of one Thomas Abeloc!

There was a general Council of the Christian Church at Lyons in 1274. Following this, at an ecclesiastical council held in Perth in 1275, Baiamundo da Vici, Canon of Asti, decreed that all beneficed clergy without exception should pay tenths of all the goods and income of their churches, according to their true value. This assessment of Scotland was merely one event in a vast scheme of Papal taxation, the purpose of which was to free the Holy Land from the Moslems. The Vicar of North Berwick was assessed for one mark!

NORTH BERWICK IN THE LATER MIDDLE AGES

DURING THE EARLIER PART of the thirteenth century, Scotland and England were at peace. But the last decade of the century showed a very different picture. By 1295 Scotland had concluded an alliance with France which was, in effect, a defensive pact against England. Then King Alexander III of Scots was killed in an accident near Kinghorn and the heir to the throne was now the "Maid of Norway". When she, too, died on her way over to her kingdom, Scotland was thrown into confusion. Eventually, Edward I, King of England, was called in to arbitrate between the many claimants to the throne. He gave his judgment in favour of John Balliol, but Balliol proved to be too compliant to Edward for the liking of the Scottish nobles, and the forces of resistance began to gather strength, uniting the many strands and sections of the population of Scotland into one. At length, Edward, furious at this resistance, determined to eliminate Scotland and everything Scottish for ever. He held court at Berwick-on-Tweed in 1296, and issued a decree summoning every landowner in Scotland to come and swear allegiance to him; he did this out of his conviction that he, Edward, was John Balliol's feudal overlord, and that therefore Balliol's kingdom belonged to him. Many did as Edward wanted, and among them was Waldeve, Vicar of North Berwick, who appended his seal to the document of allegiance, the "Ragman Roll".

But if the Vicar of North Berwick acceded to Edward's demands, it must not be thought that North Berwick held no element of resistance in the War of Independence which speedily followed, and which lasted until 1328, when by the Treaty of Northampton, Scottish independence was acknowledged. In this war, Scotland had two great champions, Sir William Wallace and, after his death Robert the Bruce. Wallace's escapades formed the material for the songs and poems of a man of a later generation whom scholars sometimes know as Henry the

Minstrel, but who is better known as Blind Harry. Among his songs about Wallace is to be found the following passage, in which he tells about the help Wallace and his guerrilla fighters got from the North Berwick landowner, Robert Lauder. Earlier, he tells how Wallace met Lauder at Musselburgh, how they became friends and cobelligerents in the "resistance". Then he goes on:

Cetoun, Lauder and Richard off Lunde
In a gud barge thai past about be se;
Sanct Jhonstoun hawyn thair ankyr haiff thai set
Twa Inglis schippis thai tuk with outyn let
The tane thai brunt, syn stuffyt the tothir weill
With artailze, and stalwart men in steyll,
To kep the port, thar suld com na wictaill
In to that toun, nor men at mycht them waill

If translation is needed, this poem tells how Lauder and his friends set out by boat from the Forth, going north round Fife Ness and into the Tay estuary, then up-river to the harbour at Perth, where they easily captured two English ships, burning one and using the other as a fortified block-ship so that the English garrison at Perth was blockaded by river.

One of North Berwick's relics is a tombstone (or what remains of it) of a Robert Lauder. Though now only two pieces remain, the record of the inscription has remained in literature. Nisbet's "Heraldry" (eighteenth century) gives it as

HIC IACET BNS ROBERTUS LAUDER MNS DNS DE CONGLETON ET
LE BASS
QUI OBIIT MENSE MAII MCCCXI (some read MCCCCXI)

"Here lies the good Robert Lauder, great laird of Congleton and
the Bass,
who died in the month of May 1311" (some read 1411)

If the 1311 reading is the correct one, this stone may commemorate the friend and helper of Sir William Wallace.

The stone itself is of some interest. In one piece till about 200 years ago, it became broken, and for many years, only one piece, the upper one, was known. It appears in a photograph of 1928, built into the rockery in the Manse garden. It was later claimed as an antiquity, and was placed among the other stones at the old kirk at the harbour. Later still, it was removed to North Berwick Museum. Meantime, when the Abbey Farm Buildings were being dismantled, a lower portion of this same stone was found, which had been used as a building stone. This part has now joined its neighbour in the Museum.

The Lauder family were important landowners in the North Berwick area from this period onwards. Various members of that family played a distinguished part in the administration of Scottish affairs. There was an Edward de Lawedre who was Archdeacon of Lothian in 1420. In 1426, Sir Robert Lauder of the Bass was King James I's Chamberlain. There was a Robert Lauder who was a Notary in North Berwick in the sixteenth century. The Lauders of the Bass were also patrons of the "hospital of poor brothers" located by the late Dr J. S. Richardson as on the site of the present Dalrymple Garage, which catered for the destitute throughout the Middle Ages, and was served by a chaplain. As will be seen later, the Lauder family were also generous in endowing chaplaincies in the parish church in the fifteenth century.

The next known Vicar of North Berwick is Alexander. In 1302 he was witness at the ceremony at which Thomas de Kirkcudbright, Bishop of Candida Casa (Whithorn), made his obedience to the newly appointed Archbishop of York, Thomas de Corbridge, at the latter's summer palace at Burton-juxta-Beverley (now Bishop Burton) in Yorkshire. It should be explained that until 1472 when St Andrews became an Archiepiscopal See, the diocese of Candida Casa was under the Archbishop of York. Thomas de Kirkcudbright is known to have spent most of his days in England. As Alexander is designated his Clerk, we may be forgiven for doubting whether North Berwick saw much of Alexander.

In 1312 the Vicar of North Berwick was William. He figures in a document in which he pledges himself and his bay horse (Lat. *badium*) in the service of King Edward II of England.

Then, in 1348, the "Black Death" hit Scotland. Ignorant of the facts of infection, and harbouring the lice which also infested the rat population, people attributed the disease to the Devil's arrows, and so Saint Sebastian, the saint who had suffered death by arrows, was often invoked for a cure in prayer. Perhaps it is to this period that the foundation of an altar to this saint in the parish church of North Berwick is due. At all events, the graveyard round the church at the harbour would daily receive its dead. It is said that half the population of Western Europe died of the "Black Death".

By 1365, the Vicar of North Berwick had resigned. His name (in its Latin form) had been Johannes Faber — John Smith or John Wright, perhaps? — and he was succeeded by Walter Bel, Chaplain to King David II.

Vicars might come and vicars might go, but North Berwick remained, and its trade continued. Its importance as a port was recognised when in 1373 King Robert II granted to North Berwick the privileges and status of a Royal Burgh, with the right to levy the King's custom duties, with a tron (a primitive weighbridge or other weighing device) and a tronar (its operator). It was not until 1481 that North Berwick returned a member to the Scottish Parliament in Edinburgh. The coat of arms granted to the Royal Burgh has already been described earlier. North Berwick's administration as a Royal Burgh worked effectively over the 600 years till 1975 when regionalisation brought about alternative forms of local government in Scotland. The original Burgh Charter was known to have been destroyed in the hurly-burly of warfare, so on 18th September 1568, King James VI granted a replacement charter giving anew these rights and privileges which North Berwick had been enjoying since the fourteenth century. One of these specifically mentioned is the right "as they have been accustomed in time past" to have a market-cross, and to have a market there every Wednesday, for the sale of "leather, skins, wool and other merchandise". In this later charter, the Burgh's boundaries are described thus:

"Beginning where Millburn enters the sea, and so going up on the west side of the said Millburn to the nearest mill situated and built on Millburn, without hurt or impediment to the aqueduct of the said mill, and so going up the bray towards the west where the drop falls from the top thereof beyond wall and ditch, and so passing towards our said burgh of North Berwick, between the top of the bray towards the west where the drops fall or may fall, and between the said bray and the sea till it comes towards the west to the burgh roods of the said town on the east and south parts, between the vennel called Kay's Wynd, next the regality of North Berwick, on the west, and the sea on

26

the north parts; and with the rock aforesaid called Craigleith, haven and custom thereof, as freely as in our said burgh. . . ."

During this fourteenth century, the state of the Church as it dominated life and thought in Western Europe had become such that people were no longer happy with an organisation in which there was now so much which was unjust, and was a mere exercise of power. This was the age of John Wyclif and his translation of the Bible into English, and his preachers, or Lollards, whose influence was felt as far north as Ayrshire. Given the words and thoughts of Jesus Christ from the pages of the gospels, how could people fail to see through the abuses and corruptions in the church? For the purposes of this history, there were in particular five types of abuse regarding appointments to office within the church:

(a) The holding of more than one office at a time by one person (Pluralism).
(b) The purchase of an office for a consideration of money (Simony).
(c) The appointment to office of relations or favoured persons (Nepotism).
(d) The appointment of a minor to an office, so that the parent or guardian of the child could reap the benefit.
(e) Deliberate failure to make an appointment so that the emoluments of the office may remain with the appointing party.

To make matters worse, in 1378 the Church in Western Europe was split asunder, and the population was treated to the appalling spectacle of two Popes, one in Rome and an Anti-Pope in Avignon, each claiming to be the true Vicar of Christ, each making appointments of priests, bishops, abbots and the like for a consideration, and each denouncing the other. This lasted until 1418. England supported the Pope of Rome. Scotland, still anxious to preserve the French connection, supported the Avignon Anti-Popes. Correspondence and money flowed freely from Scotland to Avignon, where the Anti-Popes confirmed the appointments of many individuals in their offices — priests in their parishes, bishops in their sees, abbots in their monasteries, and so on.

Among this throng is to be found the name of one William

of Norberwik who on 12th October 1380 was granted the "perpetual vicarage of Norberwik". Also known as William de Lundie, he was the most colourful character in the mediaeval history of the town. The evidence shows him to be no meek man of God, but, after the fashion of his time, worldly, ambitious, wealthy, associating with the nobility and having the ear of royalty. While petitioning Avignon for the vicarage of "Norberwik", this uninhibited pluralist was already priest of Auchindore, in the diocese of Aberdeen. He was also collated (confirmed) as Vicar of Carele (Crail, in Fife) in 1389. His alias, William de Lundie, suggests that he was also Vicar of Lundie (Lundin Links, Fife). Further, as events later proved, he was no inexperienced tenderfoot when clad in armour and wielding his axe in the thick of battle. From the pen of Jean Froissart, a French chronicler engaged in recording deeds of valour, a full account is given of William's gallant conduct on the field of Otterburn (1388). Froissart says:

> "The young Earl of Douglas had this night performed wonders in arms. When he was struck down, there was a great crowd round him; and he could not raise himself for the blow on his head was mortal. His men had followed him as closely as they were able; and there came to him his cousins Sir James Lindsay, Sir John and Sir Walter Sinclair, with other knights and squires. They found by his side a gallant knight that had constantly attended him, who was his chaplain, and had at this time exchanged his profession for that of a valiant man at arms. The whole night he had followed the Earl with his battle-axe in hand, and had by his exertions more than once repulsed the English. This conduct gained the thanks of his countrymen, and turned out to his advantage, for in the same year he was promoted to the archdeaconry and made Canon of Aberdeen. His name was Sir William de Norbenich. To say the truth, he was well found in all his limbs to shine in battle, and was severely wounded at this combat."

Writing 140 years later, John Mayr or Major, the historian, records that William received five wounds in the battle. He continues:

> "This priest received the highest praise as a warrior. You must not marvel that I have to relate such things of priests:

for Britain can show forty thousand priests who could be matched as fighting men against a like number of men from any nation. For every small laird has one chaplain, who is no despicable soldier, and the great nobles have as many as five or six who will gird on their sword and shield and go with their lords to the field. Yet this is a fashion that I in no way approve. For inasmuch as their clerical office is of the Lord, they should spend their time in divine worship and not in warfare. Yet I do not deny that for their country or to defend their own lives, they may take up arms."

Not all the heroics and gallantry in the world, however, could conceal the fact that matters were going seriously wrong at the nunnery. By 1375 the Bishop of St Andrews had received a mandate from Avignon to have the North Berwick nunnery walled in at the expense of Beatrice the Prioress and her convent. They had, it appears, been "much molested by visits from nobles and other secular persons" and were commanded to remain strictly within the walls. In 1386 Elena de Carrick was Prioress, and in 1406, King Robert III, shortly before his death, petitioned Anti-Pope Benedict XIII on behalf of one John de Carrick for a benefice in the gift of the Prioress and Convent of North Berwick "notwithstanding that he is the son of a religious". This same John de Carrick was appointed Archdeacon of Sodor, in the diocese of the Isles, some ten years later.

The Royal Burgh received a visit from King Robert III in 1391, when his young son James, who was later to succeed to the throne as King James I of Scotland, was taken to North Berwick under a strong guard to embark for France, where the king believed his son would be safer. In fact, the young prince never reached France, as he was captured by the English off Flamborough Head and taken as a prisoner to the Tower of London where he lived for 18 years before he was allowed to return.

The fifteenth century which was now dawning brings to light what might be called "The Mysterious Case of the Vanishing Vicars". After William of North Berwick, the only vicar whose name appears on any historical document is one called James. The year is 1418, and it may be significant that this was the year of the Council of Constance which put an end to the scandal of a dual Papacy, and seemed to be promising a tightening of discipline throughout the church. For the rest of the century and for 30 years or so later, no reference can be found to a Vicar of North Berwick.

But if the Vicars vanished, worship in the parish church was strengthened by chaplains privately appointed, at altars privately endowed. To this century belong the chaplainries endowed by the Lauder family. The altar of St Mary within the south aisle of the parish church, known also as the Lady Altar, or the Mary Altar, was their special concern. At this period, the church building was extended to the north and to the south to accommodate side aisles, and the south porch, the only part now standing, will date from this time also. One of the probable reasons for this porch remaining untouched while the rest of the church in later centuries was ruinous and was being quarried for its stone, may be respect for the Lauder family and their burials there.

One example of the Lauders' munificence comes from the year 1435, when, on 4th March, Robert of Lawedar of Eddrintoun, Knight, granted

"to the Lady Awter off the parische kirk of North Berwyk and tyll Schir Androw Ferour thare serwand"

his lands within North Berwick

"in the est gate and in the west gate quareuer thai be, in the ffyrst a land quylk wes sumtyme callit Cristiane Stalpartis land; Item, a land lyand ffornentis Thom Richartsoun; Item, a land in the west gate lyand neste the comoun vennel"

the whole to belong for evermore to the said altar and priest.

The above quotations, translated are:

"to the Lady Altar of the parish church of North Berwick and to Sir Andrew Ferrier serving there"

"in the East Gate and in the West Gate wherever they be, firstly, a land which was earlier called Christian Stalparts land; Item, a land lying next Tom Richardson's; Item, a land in the West Gate lying next to the common vennel"

To this same year 1435 belongs the visit of the Papal legate Aeneas Silvius Piccolomini to Scotland, a visit which started unhappily with the wreck of his ship in a storm off the mouth of the East Lothian Tyne. At the height of the storm Aeneas prayed to St Mary to rescue him and let him reach land safely, vowing that as soon as he came ashore he would seek out the nearest church dedicated to her, and there rededicate himself to the service of God through the church. On reaching land, he had to walk over frozen ground in his bare feet till eventually he found the parish church of St Mary, Whitekirk, where he knelt in worship. This must have caused a great stir in North Berwick, though at that time not even the North Berwick people could know that Aeneas was later to become Pope Pius II. On this visit to Scotland he wrote home saying that the people of Scotland were very poor, so poor that they did not burn wood, but only a kind of black stone. When the poor people were given a bag of these black stones, they went away very happy.

This century also saw the emergence of a man who earned a European reputation as a scholar, a man of learning and a noted controversialist. In his early days he was very familiar with North Berwick, its fishing community and the birds on the Bass Rock. This is John Mayr (John Major), born at Gleghornie, within the parish of North Berwick, in the year 1469. The site of a cottage in which he was born is still pointed out. A young man of alert mind, John Mayr may have attracted the attention of the Earl of Angus, who resided at Tantallon Castle, only a short distance from Gleghornie. The Earl was the father of Gavin Douglas, who became Mayr's friend and patron. Mayr's early education was at the Grammar School of Haddington, a schooling to which he later made grateful reference. He studied at Oxford, Cambridge and Paris. It is said that he graduated Master of Arts in the College of St Barbe in 1494. He then entered the College of Montaigu which at that time was a stronghold of traditional scholastic studies. In Paris he gained a notable reputation as "the veritable chief of the Scholastic philosophy" and leader of those who opposed the rising Renaissance views of Man and God. He lectured on philosophical and theological subjects, and wrote commentaries on the works of Peter Lombard. In 1521 John Mayr wrote his "Historia Maioris Britanniae". This title contains what is probably a deliberate *double entendre*, as it can mean either "The History of the Greater Britain" (Mayr was a strong advocate of the union of the kingdoms of Scotland and England), or alternatively and simply "Mayr's History of

Britain" North Berwick people may be amused to see their town referred to in this Latin work as "Berwicium Boreale" ("the northern Berwick").

In 1518 John Mayr returned to Scotland and lectured in Glasgow, where he had John Knox among his pupils. In 1523 he was admitted to St Andrews University where, until 1525 he lectured, having among his students George Buchanan the historian, and Patrick Hamilton, who later died a martyr's death for the cause of Reformation. Then Mayr went back to Paris, to continue lecturing on philosophy and theology; but by 1534 he was back in his native Scotland again, as Provost of St Salvator's College, St Andrews, an office in which he remained till his death in 1550. In 1547 he was present in Trinity Church, St Andrews, when Knox preached his famous first public sermon in which he castigated the organised church and pressed for an immediate and radical reformation.

John Mayr was noted in his lifetime for the conservatism of his philosophy, but it is now mainly for his liberalism in politics that he is remembered. He taught that the power of kings is derived from the people, and in this he was followed by George Buchanan. Though faithful to mediaeval thinking, he denounced the ecclesiastical abuses which had for so long been marring the Church's witness. The men of the generation of the Reformers themselves looked back on him with reverence. John Knox said that Mayr's "word was then holden as an oracle in matters of religioun". But his teaching evoked the opposition of Philip Melanchthon, the Lutheran Reformer, and he was lampooned by François Rabelais, the famous French satirist.

Returning to purely local events, the boatmen of North Berwick in 1474 experienced King James III's generosity. The King's *Kervell*, a yellow frigate commanded by Sir John Barton of Leith, had come to grief in the Forth. The King's Treasurer made a payment of £3 to "the men of North Berwic that fand the Kingis Ankeris and Cabillis of his Kervell" (the men of North Berwick who found the King's anchors and cables of his "Kervell").

Meanwhile, on the continent, Reformation forces were gathering strength. Events were beginning to happen which would, with mounting pace, bring radical changes to the face of Scotland in general, and to North Berwick. So it is to these we must now turn.

THE TIMES OF THE REFORMATION

THE FIRST HALF of the sixteenth century was, for the whole of Northern Europe, a time of turmoil and change. The reader is directed to any standard historical work on this period for detailed information about the struggles leading up to the Reformation, and the realignments of loyalty, and of political policy, which resulted from these events.

For our purposes it is sufficient to point out that people generally were longing for a renewal of honour and purity of life throughout the organised church, but they were frustrated because the pressure of authority from the highest echelon of power — the Papacy — was against any change in the status quo. Papal authority, it was claimed, ranked higher than even the consensus of opinion of the entire church as represented in a General Council. So movements for reform were ruthlessly suppressed, leaders of reform were burnt as heretics, and tensions mounted with each passing year.

In East Lothian there had been violence and war. In a letter of 1529 the Archbishop of St Andrews deplored the frequent devastations of the Monastery of North Berwick and its lands, and the burning of its church.

There was trouble in the making, too, for the fabric of the parish church of North Berwick. For generations, the "red leck", a line of volcanic tufa, had acted as a barrier protecting the ground on which the church was built from the fury of the sea. This had been quarried at low tide to provide stone for the ovens in royal palaces and nobles' castles, and by this time the site of the church had been left dangerously exposed. In the 1530's, the Accounts of the Masters of Works speak of "North Berwick stanis", nineteen of which were purchased from "Walter Scot, Baxter" (baker) to build a new oven for King James V at his palace of Holyroodhouse.

But there were signs that the church locally was making some attempt, albeit belated and in the end, ineffectual, to deal with the neglect of parish worship, and the place it held in the minds of the people. On 5th January 1542, the church on the Bass was officially consecrated as the parish church of the Bass, in honour of St Baldred, by Bishop William Gibson, suffragan to David Beaton, Cardinal and Archbishop of St Andrews. Then, after more than 100 years in which no vicar is traceable in North Berwick, now suddenly the church made haste to fill the ancient vacancy. In quick succession, we find that on 8th October 1547, Sir William Sinclare as Vicar was replaced by Patrick Sinclare. Both William and Patrick Sinclare were appointed to the two parishes of North Berwick and Whitekirk. Then, the following year, 1548, Mister James Broune, Schoolmaster of Linlithgow, was appointed Vicar of North Berwick (only), but there must have been some hurried or confused arrangement, because that same year he was also appointed to the "rectoria" of Kirknewton and his place as Vicar of North Berwick (and Whitekirk) was taken by Mister Archibald Barre.

Earlier, King Henry VIII of England had marched on Scotland in 1544, and the Earl of Hertford had been sent to devastate Edinburgh and Leith. The Prioress and Nuns of North Berwick, as proprietors of the Law, were responsible for lighting a beacon on top of the Law to warn the countryside of the advance of hostile troops. Later, French troops, summoned in defence of the status quo by the opponents of the Reformation, entered East Lothian and occupied most of it as if it had been a French colony. Of the occupation of Haddington, one English observer wrote home saying "Everything here passes in the name of the King of France". Doubtless these French troops would be seen in North Berwick also.

The struggle between reforming and non-reforming parties, English-supported and French-supported parties continued. There had been martyrs to the cause of Reformation — Patrick Hamilton, widely travelled scholar and advocate of a Reformation after the Lutheran manner, was burnt in 1528: George Wishart, who went to study at Basle and Zurich, came under the influence of the Genevan reformation, was Tutor at Corpus Christi College, Cambridge, in 1543, and died a martyr's death in 1546. There was also murder. Hatred of Cardinal Beaton had risen to such a height that in the same year, just three months after Wishart's death, he was murdered.

Eventually, in August 1560, the Estates of Scotland (The Scottish Parliament) formally brought the *ancien régime* to a close, abolishing the authority of the Pope within the realm of Scotland, and placing Scotland firmly on the side of the reformed and reforming parts of the church.

Of greatest importance to North Berwick, however, in those troubled times, was neither the appointments of vicars nor the clash of arms nor the blood of the martyrs. The fact was that all the endowments of the church, given in earlier centuries by nobles as acts of faith, of piety and of charity, were being alienated to secular personages. The church, including the religious houses, was, by comparison with the average man, prodigiously wealthy. There were some families who sought to be in a position to grasp the church's lands as soon as opportunity should offer.

While this kind of thing was happening over the whole country, this process of alienation in North Berwick was dominated by the relations of the last two Prioresses, Isabella and Margaret Home, and in patricular by Alexander Home, son of Patrick Home of Polwarth, Margaret Home's brother. Over a short period of 30 years or so they dismantled between them the entire fabric of the nunnery and its endowments. On 12th August 1544, two mills of North Berwick, with their lands and with the "Myln Croft" (on the high ground to the east of the Glen) were made over to Alexander Home. In 1561, Margaret Home gave the lands of "Lamysyde and Heckilwelcros" to Andrew Home. Dr J. S. Richardson considered that Lamysyde or Lamside was the earlier name of the site on which the 1825 Manse was built. In 1562, Alexander Home was given by his aunt the Prioress the "fermelandis" with the sea shore, "the links" belonging to them. Even the King was brought into this process of dismemberment. By a charter of 1568, King James VI made over to Prioress Margaret Home all the benefice of the priory which remained in his hands by the resignation of Dame Mariot Cockburne. That same year, the Prioress turned over the Newark (the house built within the grounds of the nunnery), the house, the buildings of the nunnery (now in ruins), its dovecote, its gardens and orchards near the said monastery, to Alexander Home. The next year, 1569, all remaining lands and possessions whatsoever of the monastery were made over to Alexander

Home. Four years later, the King granted to Alexander Home a tenement of land in North Berwick which had reverted to him by the death of William Lauder, natural son of Robert Lauder of the Bass without legitimate heirs of his body.

The story of these operations cannot be finished without reference to the last Vicar of North Berwick under the church unreformed, Alexander Wood. He was the second son of Sir Andrew Wood of Largo, a naval commander who had gained considerable fame for his victory over an English naval force under Stephen Bull, off the Bell Rock, near Arbroath. Alexander Wood first appears as a witness to a charter of William, Bishop of Aberdeen, on 20th August 1556. To that year also belongs a charter in which Jonet Wod, natural daughter of Alexander Wod, Vicar of North Berwick, resigns and renounces her claim on the tiends of grain of the parish of Kilconquhar in favour of Margaret Howme, Prioress of the nunnery of North Berwick. As a tiend of victual of this sort should properly become the stipend of a Vicar of Kilconquhar, assuming that there was one appointed, it is clear that Margaret Home and Alexander Wood were and had been treating such matters as family affairs, and this at once raises the question what the relationship was between Vicar of North Berwick and the Prioress. By 5th December 1557, Alexander Wood is "M. Alexander Wod, vicar pensioner of North Berwick" who grants his croft to Alexander Carrick, burgess of North Berwick. As Alexander Home had done with the nunnery's endowments south of the Forth, so Alexander Wood did with those on the Fife side. By 1559 he is described in a charter as Vicar of Largo, and on March 10th that year he married his natural daughter Alison Wod to the Alexander Carrick to whom he had granted his vicar's croft two years previously. On 21st May 1573 he is described as "M. Alexander Wod de Grange" and has been granted the "Erlisferry", with its harbour and anchorages and the right of ferry. Two years later, "Robert Wod, bastard, natural son of Alexander Wod of Grange" received letters of legitimation from the King.

As far as the actual work done by the Vicar of North Berwick was concerned, it is clear from a charter of 1554 that parish work was being performed by a duly appointed curate, acting in place of the vicar. His name was Sir George Lyell. No record remains of what happened to parish worship at the time of the Reformation, but we need no specially good imagination to conclude that, as happened everywhere else in Scotland, the images of the saints would be destroyed. This appears to be the one precept of the reformers which was faithfully carried out with zeal by what John Knox called "the rascal multitude". The altar of St Mary in the parish church which had been endowed by the Lauders of the Bass, had given its name to that part of the church as the Lady Aisle. After the Reformation, traditional sainthood being no longer material, the name might pass easily through the form "the Lady of Bass's Aisle" (the reference now being to the family of Lauder of the Bass) into the form "the Laird of Bassis Aisle", which is the form found in the following century.

The new regime in the church started with some hesitancy. The old authorities of Pope, Archbishop and Bishop had gone. The new conciliar form of church government, imported from Geneva, took some time to come into effective operation. It was not until 1567 that North Berwick had its Minister after the reformed pattern. His name was John Young, but he was succeeded only one year later by Patrick Creich. Not until 1587 was the Manse and Glebe of North Berwick officially delineated by the Presbytery. By that time, the nunnery buildings had been razed to the ground, and the nunnery church with them, being "no paroche kirke". Alexander Home, now known as the "Gudeman of North Berwick" was in possession of the lands of North Berwick as a barony, and held the right of "patronage to the parsonage and vicarage of the Paroche Kirk of North Berwick".

The images of the saints were down. The Mass was proscribed. The church, once rich, was now poor. By 1592, the nunneries and monasteries were officially suppressed. The Pope's authority was abolished. No pilgrims to St Andrews, no preaching friars, were to be seen. In North Berwick, as elsewhere in Scotland, the Middle Ages had gone for ever.

SPEAK OF THE DEVIL

EARLIER CHAPTERS may leave the impression that in North Berwick at least, whatever may have been the case elsewhere, the one and only religion, and the one and only way of thinking, was Christianity. While without question the life of the people was dominated by Christian concepts from birth to death, as interpreted by the church of the time, it is also true that there was an under-current of religion and life which owed little or nothing to Christianity. Certain features of this alternative religion have been remarkably resistant to time's erosion. As late as 1952 when the author came to North Berwick, there were still members of the fishing community who, half in jest, but equally half in earnest, would tell him that while on board a boat, there were certain words which were forbidden. One must not refer to salmon or pigs or hares. Conversation about these was carefully avoided. If it was utterly necessary to refer to them, it must be by circumlocution — "the pink yins" for salmon, "the grumphy yins" for pigs, and "the lang-leggit yins" or "the lang-eared yins" for hares. A minister or a priest of the Christian church was a figure to be avoided, especially in earlier days, it was said, and as for a nun — she was most of all to be avoided. A fisherman on his way to take his boat out on a fishing trip, if he met a minister, would turn back and not go out that day. To go out would only be to court bad luck. Alternatively, he could put his cap round back-to-front, and go ahead. This, symbolically, would deceive the powers in the Other World into thinking that he was going THIS way, when in fact he was going THAT way, and if they were preparing bad luck for him, they would prepare it somewhere along THIS way, when in fact of course he was really going THAT way.

Such superstitions must have had their origins in the religion which preceded the coming of Christianity, an animistic religion which saw spirits in animals and in inanimate objects — spirits which could be hurtful if not treated respectfully. During the Christian centuries such a religion had led an underground existence, and by the sixteenth century it had become intermingled with other elements. The first of these is what in modern days we call Extra-Sensory Perception, and to it we could add any other manifestation of psychic activity — water-divining, poltergeists, psychic healing, necromancy and the like. The second of these other elements might be the traditional learning of the women of the Middle Ages about herbs, particularly those associated with help at times of woman's special need — menstruation (and non-menstruation), pregnancy, childbirth, and the menopause. There is one further ingredient which in this sixteenth century is prominent — a perversity which sought to worship evil rather than good, which denied Christ and all things Christian, and led a follower to renounce his baptism and his baptismal name in favour of pagan alternatives.

Out of such a list of ingredients, in varying proportion, arose the witchcraft of East Lothian which we meet in the famous episode of the Devil and the Witches at North Berwick Kirk. Witches were no new thing. It was the use to which they were put on this occasion that was novel.

King James VI had been spending the summer of 1590 in Denmark, wooing and winning his bride, Princess Anne of Denmark. He had a suite of rooms given by the King of Denmark in Kronborg Castle at Elsinore (Hälsingör), north of Copenhagen. This in fact was the castle made famous by Shakespeare in Hamlet. While the king was absent from Scotland, Francis Stuart, Earl of Bothwell, had been leading a conspiracy against him and his bride. This Francis Stuart was the illegitimate grandson of James V, James VI's grandfather. He had always been something of an *enfant terrible* and was a convinced believer in the witch's art. Such evidence as there is in the North Berwick "happening" suggests that Francis was motivated by a desire to get the King and his bride out of the way, believing that he could by witchcraft raise a storm in the estuary of the Forth, thus hopefully to wreck the king's ship with both its royal occupants as they sailed into home waters.

As it was told at the trial later, the witches of East Lothian, about 200 in number, were summoned to meet the Devil at the Kirk of North Berwick. It also appeared that this was not the first time they had so met. There had been other meetings at North Berwick, and at Prestonpans. Clearly, the "Devil" was none other than Francis Stuart himself, suitably disguised with black cloak, black leather face-mask, and tail. We may assume that his reason for choosing North Berwick was the wide and commanding view of the sea, and of all incoming craft. If the King's ship were to arrive in the Forth, it would come within range, so to speak, of Francis Stuart's supernatural powers.

Some of the witches came from the country farms and crofts within a radius of about 15 to 20 miles. Others, it was said, came by sea, sailing on sieves (or riddles, as used in agriculture) which they had bewitched so that they could float. As they sailed, they made merry with flagons of wine. When they arrived, all the witches joined hands and danced a reel, while a girl called Gilles Duncan accompanied them on a Jew's Harp. In passing, the author believes that this girl's first name, so written, is an attempt to write the name Dilais, a Gaelic name meaning faithful and pronounced Jee-las — a small indication, perhaps, of lingering Gaelic influence in sixteenth century East Lothian.

As Gilles played, the witches sang their processional song —

> Commer goe ye before
> Commer goe ye
> Gif ye will not go before
> Commer let me

When they arrived at the church, one of the witches, John Cunningham, who in everyday life was the schoolmaster at Prestonpans, "blew up the doors and blew in the lights". Then the "Devil" leapt up into the pulpit, and called the roll. The witch-name, not the baptismal name, would be used. John Cunningham was known as Doctor Fian (again Gaelic — the white one?), and he was the "Devil"'s Clerk or Secretary. As each name was called, the reply came, "Here, Maister".

When all were present and correct, the "Devil" asked what evil they had done since they last met, and how many converts to the witch's art they had made. Some had made a wax effigy of King James, and at a previous meeting at Prestonpans, the "Devil" had pronounced sentence of death upon it. Now he wanted to know what effect this had had on the King. When one poor ploughman present was heard to reply "There is naething ails the King yet, God be thankit," the "Devil" struck him a hard blow. When some others expressed surprise that for all their devilry, no harm had come to the King, the "Devil" explained "Il est un homme de Dieu" — He is a man of God, and God has protected him.

Following this, on the "Devil's" instructions, the company "opened the graves, twa within and ane without the kirke, and took off the joints of the corpses' fingers, taes and knees" and parted them among them. He commanded them to keep the joints on their persons until they were dry, and then to make a powder with them, "to do evil withal".

As the proceedings drew to a close, the company did their final obeisance to the "Devil". The element of perversity is here shown clearly in that, instead of kissing his hand, the company were made to kiss his bare buttocks, which he exposed over the pulpit. Those who did so said they were as cold as ice and as hard as iron.

Yet in spite of all the ceremonies and spells, the King and his bride arrived back in safety. When King James got to know what had happened, he insisted on being present personally at the witch-trial which followed, and he questioned some of the witnesses. These included "Agnes Sampson, of Haddington", "Agnes Tompson, of Edenbrough", and "Doctor Fian" already mentioned. Having heard their testimony he declared that they were "all extreame lyars". Francis Stuart, for his part, denied any part in the affair, and voluntarily put himself under the protection of the King in Edinburgh Castle. He was willing, he said, to stand trial and rebut the accusations of witchcraft and conspiracy implied in common rumour. The King was unwilling to believe any evil of him, but others put the story about that Francis' life was in danger. Hearing this, he escaped from the castle. Shortly after this, he made another attempt on the King's life, this time at Holyroodhouse, but this also was unsuccessful, and he is said to have escaped to Italy, to return later to this country, still practising the black arts.

By way of epilogue to this strange affair, the following might be said:

    (1) The year after the North Berwick event, a "horror-comic" was published in London, entitled "Newes from Scotland", in which the whole story of the witches and the Devil was told, with woodcut illustrations which were imaginative rather than realistic, but which have become associated with this story ever since.

    (2) Though God's wrath did not descend on North Berwick

Kirk in 1590, a ferocious storm did happen about 60 years later, when the church was reduced to ruins.

(3) The North Berwick witches became famous overnight, and were absorbed into the body of Scottish legend. Robert Burns who lived nearly 200 years after these events, must have heard about them and used them in composing his world-famous and hilarious tale of Tam-o'-Shanter and the witches at the Old Kirk at Alloway. Captain Francis Grose, a friend of Robert Burns, knew about the North Berwick witches, and included a sketch of the ruined church of North Berwick as it was in his day, in his book "Antiquities of Scotland".

(4) May there not be a connection between the North Berwick witches and the doctrine of the Divine Right of Kings which in a later generation made such trouble for the Stuart Kings? King James was extremely interested in two things — the kingship and the power of the occult, as evidenced by his published writings — his *Basilikon Doron* and his *Demonology*. Might he not have considered that he, knowing who his personal enemies were and knowing also that he had got them under control, had now only to get to know what unseen powers there were which might threaten his throne? Coming to the conclusion that the witches were all "extreme lyars" and that the worst they could do, even with the help of the Prince of Darkness himself, could not take his throne from him, would not the way be clear for him to develop in his mind the thought that by God's will, nothing whatsoever in heaven or on earth could interfere with his royal status and will?

(5) The voyage of the ships to and from Denmark had an unfortunate sequel. From a "complaint" (petition) to the Privy Council dated 7th April 1613, we learn that the burghs of Montrose, Brechin, Dunbar, Northberwick, Elgin, Inverness, Forres, Nairn, Tain and Cullen were to give 3,000 merks between them for the expenses of one of the ships, which ship was to be provided by the burgh of Aberdeen; North Berwick's share was £18 3s. 7d. and Dunbar's £36 7s. 4d. George Knowis, burgess of Aberdeen, had advanced the whole 3,000 merks and was given authority to collect the

burghs' shares within a certain time. All this had been done without the consent of the other burghs. North Berwick and Dunbar complained that this was unjust — also, that as a result of the arrangement, Aberdeen would pay nothing (having supplied the use of the ship) and that any profit on the deal would go to Aberdeen. As the boat had done its work, had gone to Denmark and had returned, all within 20 days, all the burghs should have to pay should be, at the most, one month's hire of the boat. Comparison was made with the boat supplied by Edinburgh ("quhilk was of a gritter birth and far better apparelit nor the bark of Abirdene") which cost only £800. North Berwick lodged £30 in court plus "obedience" of £24 11s. "in case the said George Knowis aught to have the same". In the end, the Lords of the Privy Council gave judgment for the pursuers.

"Doctor Fian" and friend ride to the great meeting of witches at the church of North Berwick

(Newes from Scotland, 1591)

43

THE SEVENTEENTH CENTURY

IN 1603, on the death of Queen Elizabeth Tudor of England, King James VI of Scotland succeeded to her throne, thus in his person creating a United Kingdom of England and Scotland. This was a development of importance in British history, and it was not unimportant from the point of view of James himself, of Scotland, and of Edinburgh. For James, it meant that he now ruled a vastly greater kingdom: for Scotland, that perpetual war with England was now a thing of the past: and for Edinburgh, that the king and the court had left for London, Holyroodhouse was empty, and the first step had been taken in the decline of the "Royal Mile".

But North Berwick had not lost its loyalty to, nor its concern for, the king. In 1604 the first known book of minutes of the Kirk Session of North Berwick starts, and one of its early entries reads —

Rex
Nov. 5
1605
The fyft of november being tuysday the Lord of his grett mercie preserved our king and quenes Maties the prince and Rest of the nobilitie quha wer to accumpany ther Maties to the parliament houss the said day frome ane wonderfull and devilish stratagem devisit be Satan and his instruments, to haif destroyit ther Majesties and nobles be blawing upp the houss quherin they suld haif bene at parliament wt barrells and huggetts of puldre lyid in the nether houss to that effect.

The holder of the barony of North Berwick had been Alexander Home, "the Gudeman of North Berwick", but now he was dead, and Sir John Home held the title. As his predecessor had done, he held the right of presentation of a minister to the parish church. But by now, relations between laird and minister had soured. On 29th January 1607, the Privy Council in Edinburgh were required to arbitrate in a dispute between Sir John Home of North Berwick and Mr John Adamson, minister at North Berwick. It appeared that there had been "injurie and offence alledgit committit be the said Sir Johnne againis the said Mr Johnne Adamsoun, by the uttering of injurious and dispytfull speitches aganis him, being his ordinair pastour, and stryking of him with his fauldit neve (clenched fist) upoun the face". The matter of "satisfaction" claimed by the minister was referred to a panel of arbiters, four in number, two for Sir John and two for Mr Adamson, with an "oversman" (neutral chairman) in the person of "Johnne, Archbishop of Glasgow".

In passing, this serves as a reminder that this was the first of two periods in the history of the Church of Scotland when there were bishops as well as presbyteries.

In 1621, the Archbishop of St Andrews was involved in another difficult case regarding the appointment of a minister to North Berwick parish. By this time, the right of presentation had passed into the hands of the king, and his nominee had been one Michael Gilbert. The Commissioners from North Berwick, appointed by the Presbytery, however, reported "in the name of the whole people, that thei were not content with Michael Gilbert, and that universallie ye people had no lyking for him, and thawcht not meet for that places". Thereafter, the Presbytery "commends and allows his gift and holie effectioun, juges him able to enter in the ministrie, qr. it sall please God to call him with consent of the congregation but in respect of the place of North Berwick qr. unto the Generall Assemblie holdin at Aberdeen has thawcht meit, an man of singular gifts and authoritie, and experience. Also in respect of ye commissionars of ye said parochin of North Berwick dissenting yr fra, we think him not meit for yt. place of North Berwick."

But though the Presbytery resolved not to proceed with the appointment, yet after considerable delay, the Archbishop gave authority for Michael Gilbert to be settled: and so it transpired. Michael Gilbert was Minister of North Berwick for six years.

North Berwick events might have, at this period, little more than purely local significance. But there is some evidence that Scotland generally was becoming slightly better known, slightly less of a *terra incognita* than before. Some time about the beginning of the seventeenth century, an early Scottish cartographer, Timothy Pont, had made a Scottish Atlas. Framed copies of his map of East Lothian are still popular as wall pictures in houses today. This was followed in 1610 by a map of Scotland by John Speed. In Speed's map, "N. Barwik" is shown, and off shore, "Crag lyth" and "The Basse". But what is S. Koldes? Could this be Scoughall? And what is "Fommgen" where Tyninghame might be?

This century saw the visits to East Lothian of at least two men who have left records of what they saw. The first of these was John Taylor, writer of "The Pennyless Pilgrimage, or the Moneyless Perambulation of John Taylor, alias the King's Majesties Water-Poet: How he travailed on foot from London to Edenborough in Scotland, not carrying any money to and fro, neither Begging, Borrowing, or asking Meate, Drinke, or Lodging" (1618). He tells how, at "Adam" (=Auldhame) "Master John Acmootye his house" (the name would be Auchmithie), he was well entertained:

> "Amongst our viands that wee had there, I must not forget the soleand goose, a most delicate fowle, which breeds in great abundance in a little rocke called the Basse, which stands two miles into the sea. It is very good flesh, but it is eaten in the forme as wee eate oysters, standing at a sideboord, a little before dinner, unsanctified without grace; and after it is eaten, it must be well liquored with two or three good rowses of sherrie or Canarie sacke. The lord or owner of the Basse doth profit at the least two hundred pound yeerly by those geese; the Basse itselfe being of a great height, and neere three quarters of a mile in compasse, all fully replenished with wildfowle, having but one small entrance into it, with a house, a garden and a chappel in it: and on the toppe of it a well of pure fresh water."

North Berwick and the Bass had a very distinguished visitor some years later, in the person of Dr William Harvey, the discoverer of the circulation of the blood. Writing in 1651, he tells of a visit to the Bass:

> "There is a small island the Scots call the Bass Island . . . situated in the open ocean, not far from the shore, of the most abrupt and precipitous character, so that it resembles some huge rock or stone more than an island; indeed it is no more than a mile in circumference. The surface of this island in the months of May and June is almost covered with nests, eggs and young birds, so that you can scarcely find free footing anywhere; and then such is the density of the flight of the old birds above, that, like a cloud, they darken the sun and the sky, and such the screaming and

46

Ruins of buildings associated with the fortress on Bass Rock (before 1902)

Ruins of fortress on Bass Rock (before 1902)

din, that you scarce hear the voice of one who addresses you. . . . There is one feature I shall mention — and it also bears me out in my report of the multitudes of sea-fowl — the whole island appears of a brilliant white colour; to those who approach it, all the cliffs look as if they consisted of white chalk. The true colour of the rock is dusky and black. It is a friable white crust that is spread over, and which gives the island its whiteness and splendour — a crust having the same consistency, colour and nature as an eggshell, which plasters everything with a hard though friable and testaceous kind of covering. The lower part of the rock, laved by the ebbing and flowing tide, preserves its native colour, and clearly shows that the whiteness of the superior parts is due to the liquid excrement of the birds which are voided along with the alvine faeces; which liquid excrements — white, hard, and brittle, like the shell of an egg — cover the rock, and under the influence of the cold air encrust it."

In France at this period, La Rochelle had fallen, and the Protestants there were in a pitiful state, Their distress had become known throughout the Reformed world, and they became an object of charitable appeal. The church in Scotland gave money to relieve them, of which the Presbytery of Haddington gave £2,302 Scots. This included a contribution from North Berwick of £88 14s. 4d., and this was handed over to representatives of the Reformed Churches in France and the "Souveranatie of Bearn" in Edinburgh on 23rd March 1622. La Rochelle itself became popularly known in Scotland as "the Rotchell" and has given its name to a locality in Maxwelltown, Dumfries.

The year 1633 saw the end of the Home family's tenure of the lands of North Berwick. In this year Patrick, fifth Baron Home, sold the estate to Sir William Dick of Braid, merchant and burgess in Edinburgh, who was Provost of Edinburgh from 1638 to 1640. This was not the first, and as we shall see, it was not the last, connection between North Berwick and the Provosts of Edinburgh. As early as 1594 the Provost of Edinburgh at that time had a house in North Berwick. The Dick family, and the Lauder family mentioned in an earlier chapter, are commemorated in the names of two residential streets in the Grange district in Edinburgh — Dick Place and Lauder Road.

Later in the century, Sir William Dick fell into financial difficulties and the estate was confiscated by the Commissioners for the Commonwealth. Sir William Dick himself died before 20th July 1659.

While the North Berwick estate was changing hands, the parish minister of North Berwick was succeeding in strengthening his financial position. In 1633 he received a re-augmentation of his stipend from the Parliamentary Commissioners. The church itself could afford a new bell by 1642. This bell, which now rests at the foot of the tower stairs in the present St Andrew's Church, was cast by James Monteith in Edinburgh. In addition to the Scottish thistle, it bears the emblem of the Edinburgh Guild of Hammermen, and the legend:

JACOBUS MONTEITH ME FECIT EDINB UGH PRO TEMPLO DE
NORTHBERWICK 1642 SPERO MELIORA

("James Monteith made me in Edinburgh for the church of
North Berwick — 1642 — I hope for better things").

This bell would be mounted in the tower at the parish church at the harbour, and would ring there for the few years left for the life of that building. Later, it was transferred to the tower of the second church, and then in 1907 when the tower of the present St Andrew's Church was completed, it was hung there. It is cracked, however, and while the story put about at the time speaks of it being cracked "through age", an unofficial story tells of a workman involved in the labour of hanging the bell, who, impatient with the strains and frustrations of the work, struck the bell, newly hung, with a sledgehammer, and cracked it. What age alone could not do, age plus violence accomplished. Yet the bell rang in its cracked state from 1907 to 1928, when it was replaced by the present bell, cast of metal gifted by Mr John Menzies, of station bookstall fame.

To return to the seventeenth century, the church had by this time in operation a system of relief of the poor. As in other parishes, there would be collections in church for the poor. Fines for offences dealt with by the Kirk Session would go to the poor; and there might be, in some parishes, monies mortified (permanently invested) whose annual rent (interest) would likewise help the poor. On the expenditure side, it was a matter of careful concern that the widows of the parish should each receive an appropriate and regular monthly remittance — not much, because the church was poor and depended on the givings of the people for such matters, but enough to make the difference between survival and death. There was consideration given also to the wandering poor and casual charity. A small iron box dating from this period, rediscovered among church papers some 20 years ago or so, may have been designed to deal with contributions to these funds. It has four latches and four locks, and so cannot be opened unless all four keys are used. It is at present in the Vestibule of St Andrew's parish church.

By the late 1640's however, there seems to have been concern over the fabric of the parish church at the harbour. Wind and wave, combined with the removal of the protection afforded by the "red leck" must have begun their work of undermining the church. Yet the church building itself still remained unharmed on 27th June 1649 when the Presbytery stated "The fabrik of the Kirk is in nothing found defective". But disaster was near at hand. Some time between then and 23rd October 1656 the building had become a ruin. The church had lost its eastern end, cut off by a line running diagonally across the crossing approximately south-east to north-west, the graveyard east of the church had been washed away, and the site was now unfit for use as a place of worship. The bridge, too, which attached the harbour island to the mainland, had been swept away. The Presbytery received a petition from the "Burrough of North Berwick for help to erect their bulwark". The Kirk Session resolved rather to change the site of North Berwick's parish church than to rebuild the church and the bridge.

Controversy then arose about the site of the future church and graveyard. Some favoured a site at Harelaw, or at Bonnington. The laird of "Bagoon" (Balgone) held out for the Heugh. These facts come as a reminder to our urban generation that at that time North Berwick was only a tiny village settlement set on the northern edge of a large agricultural parish, and that the countryside was much more populous than at present. Again, there were others who favoured a site nearer the centre of the township. Meantime, emergency arrangements had to be made to accommodate the parishioners for Sunday worship. It was here that Sir Andrew Dick (heir of the late Sir William Dick) came to the rescue by allowing the use of his "great tenement or Lodgeing lying within the burgh of North

49

Berwick" for "preaching". The boundaries of this property make it clear that the site is that now occupied by the Dalrymple Arms Hotel in Quality Street. The Kirk Session Book describes it as "the hous wher sermon is". These references also elucidate for a modern reader how deeply the reformation doctrine of the Priesthood of all Believers had cut. Real worship on a day-to-day basis was no longer a matter for a daily service in church. It was now in the hands of the male head of each family. Each father was to be a priest to his family circle and servants, and conduct daily family worship in his own house. A church was then only for use as a place where the Word of God might be expounded and the Sacrament of the Lord's Supper celebrated. The central focus of Sunday worship then became the minister's sermon; and this is an emphasis which has for long remained in the Reformed tradition, even though times later changed so much that daily family worship conducted by the father of each family — the justification for this emphasis — completely vanished.

One other consequence of this doctrine concerned the design of churches. Before the Reformation, cross-shaped churches were divided into two sections by a Rood Screen. Within the choir or chancel the ordained priesthood and their assistants might celebrate the Sacraments, while the laity occupied the nave. But now, under Reformation thinking, the clergy/laity division made nonsense, if all believers were priests. So then all believers might occupy the choir. And if all occupied the choir, what need was there for nave or transepts? Accordingly, we find churches of this immediate post-Reformation period in Scotland taking the form of oblong buildings, with the pulpit placed in the middle of the long side, as if the building were the choir of a cross-church. The doctrine was taken to its logical conclusion when box-pews were erected in such churches, giving a small area to each of the heritors — in the North Berwick case, these were the Burgh, and proprietors of land within the parish, collectively responsible for paying for capital expenditure and running repairs on the fabric of the church building. So, in theory at least, there was a place for everyone in the church — Town Council, burgesses and inhabitants of the Burgh, the landed proprietors, their tenant farmers and families, their farm workers, servants and helpers of every sort.

Such was the prevailing thinking which faced North Berwick in its search for a new church. In the end, the party who

Early photograph of North Berwick Parish Church. Note the Session House, Vestibule with internal stairway, and access to the Dalrymple loft by external stairway

North Berwick Parish Church, some time in the late 1870's, after the painting by W. E. Lockhart, R.S.A. In the laird's loft are Sir Hew Dalrymple (sixth baronet) and Lady Dalrymple

favoured a town site won, and land was purchased, south of the High Street properties and their gardens to the rear. The site thus obtained was then levelled to provide a suitable graveyard for the dead of the parish, and the building of the church began. Stone from the earlier church was used, and also stone from the Law quarry which gives the church its characteristic reddish colour. The plan of the building followed the accepted norm — an oblong building with the pulpit in the centre of the long side. In its final form, the church possessed four "lofts", one at either end, and a loft for each of the two major landed proprietors — the holders of the Barony of North Berwick (the Dalrymple family as from 1694) and the Sutties (later, the Grant-Sutties) of Balgone. According to oral tradition still current in this century, the pulpit was a double one, with an upper rear section for the minister, and a lower front section for the precentor. There is, in North Berwick Museum, an oil painting of the interior of this church as it was in the latter years of last century. The painter, W. E. Lockhart, R.S.A., had relations who lived in North Berwick, and it is said that the people shown in the picture were painted from life, but individually, and the resultant picture is a pastiche. Care has been taken to ensure that it is as realistic a representation of the interior of the church as possible. This picture was very kindly given to the Parish Church of St Andrew by the late Sir Hew Dalrymple — the ninth baronet.

For the building of the church, timber — "trees" and "dails" — had to be imported, and slates, over which a guard had to be posted, as there had been losses due to pilfering!

When the total cost was reckoned up, it came to approximately £2,400 Scots, or £200 Sterling.

It was not until the summer of 1664 that the building was ready for use as the parish church. On 5th June that year, the Session Book states simply "This day the paroch mett for worship in ye new kirke". A sundial bearing the date 1680 was added later. The new graveyard was ready also, but where a deceased's family held ground in the graveyard at the harbour church, burials continued in those parts so far untouched by the waves, for a very long time. As late as the 1830's there were burials there, but on 7th January 1672, the Kirk Session resolved:

"that who should after the dait of thir presents burie in the old kirke yeard should pay twentie shillings Scotts for sand

and faill, least the coffin should againe be discovered by winde and weather".

The thoroughfare now known as Kirk Ports was created at this time also so that horse-drawn transport might conveniently get from one end to the other of the little burgh without passing through the High Street or trespassing on the graveyard.

But while North Berwick appeared peaceful about this time, there was unrest and violence in the larger world outside. The Covenanting movement, emphasising the freedom of the Christian against the pressures of earthly authoritarianism, was doing battle against royal authority in the church and its backing of military force. One of those caught up in this conflict was John Blackadder, parish minister of Troqueer, a parish lying across the River Nith from the town of Dumfries. Born in 1615 at Blairhall, near Culross in Fife, he became a successful minister with a parish who followed and honoured him. He taught that the prelatic system of church government, for which Charles II's regime stood, was, by God's word, unlawful; and that presbyterianism was of divine right. He publicly objected to the consecration of bishops in the Church of Scotland, particularly by the hands of those who went to England to be consecrated there. One thing led to another, and John Blackadder found himself "outed" from his parish in 1662. He and his family found temporary refuge in the mansion house of Barndennoch, the property of Lady Craigdarroch. But being "outed" he now had the whole of the south of Scotland for his "parish". He settled in Edinburgh, but spent most of his time travelling on horseback preaching and celebrating the Sacraments and giving support to those who attended the open-air conventicles. From 1669 to 1681 his services were in great demand, and his reputation as a wanted man increased. At length he was arrested in Edinburgh on 5th April 1681, charged with preaching in the fields. The government had got their man, and Blackadder was sentenced to imprisonment on the Bass Rock. Conditions there were unspeakable. Food was bad and water was scarce. The rooms of the prison, writes his son John, were "ordinarily full of smoke, like to suffocate and choke them, so as my father and the other prisoners were necessitate many a time to thrust head and shoulders out of the window to recover breath". Yet in these conditions John Blackadder wrote his Memoirs. He died on the Bass in 1685, aged 70, and as the Bass

"Goodall's Corner" — *High Street, looking east about 1900*

Appeal for funds to build a Free Church in North Berwick (Blackadder Church) (1843)

now lay within the parish of North Berwick, he was buried in the graveyard of the new parish church.

John Blackadder's significance for North Berwick was not at an end, however, with his death. When in 1843 the Church of Scotland was rent in two over the question of the appointment of parish ministers by the system of Patronage, the party in North Berwick which favoured the formation of a Free Church in the town (i.e., free from the pressure of secular authority upon church affairs) claimed that the principles for which they were now standing were virtually the same as those for which John Blackadder worked and died, that they would build a church in North Berwick and call it Blackadder Church. This they did, and Blackadder Church has retained its name to the present day, within a reunited Church of Scotland.

Four years after the death of John Blackadder, another divisive issue began making its mark on Scottish life — Jacobitism. By the "Revolution Settlement" of 1688 the throne of the United Kingdom passed to William of Orange and to Mary, his Queen. But there were many who disliked and opposed this, and supported the descendents of James II of the United Kingdom. This division is seen in North Berwick for the first time when the Privy Council had to deal with the Minister of North Berwick, Mr Andrew Guild, for his refusal to pray for King William and Queen Mary. Arrayed against the minister on this occasion was a deputation representing the parishioners, and, to represent the King's interest, Sir John Dalrymple, younger, of Stair. The Privy Council, in its judgment of 27th August 1689, declares that all subjects are "ingadged to pray for their lawfull soveraigne; and particularly by ane act of the Meitting of the Estates of the date the thretein day of Apryle jmviceightie nyne years all ministers who are in ane eminent maner obleidged to discharge that bound dutie are thereby expresslie commanded to read a proclaimatione of that date and publictly to pray for King William and Queen Mary as King and Queen of this realme upon the dayes particularlie therin mentionit under the paine of being deprived and lossing of ther benefices, and that by that same proclaimatione all the leidges are certified that they presume not to owne or acknowledge the late King James the Seventh for their King or presume upon their highest perrill by word, wryting, in sermons or any other maner of way to impunge or disowne the royall authoritie of William and Mary as King and Queen of Scotland".

The minute continues to tell that Mr Andrew Guild had neither read the proclamation nor prayed for King William and Queen Mary. When asked point-blank "if he was yet willing to read (the proclamation) nixt Sabboth" he replied "that he hade not read the samen at any tyme becaus he hade some scrouples and was not free as yet to read the samen" whereupon, the Privy Council deprived him of his benefice "at the said Kirk of North Berwick", declared the charge vacant, and "ordaines him to remove from his manss and gleib at the term of Mertimiss nixt".

In June 1691 some men of the Jacobite forces under General Buchan who had been captured at a skirmish at Cromdale in 1690, were sent under guard to the Bass Rock, to live in the prison cells lately occupied by the Covenanters. Their leader was a Captain Middleton. Within a few weeks of their arrival, while a coal boat was being unloaded, they turned the tables on their captors, overpowered the sentry, shut the gates and captured the armoury. This Jacobite occupation of the Bass continued until 18th April 1694. By that time, although they had been living a piratical life, stealing food nightly from the mainland, they were at the end of their resources, and the Jacobite cause appeared to them to be finally lost. But when the government party arrived to negotiate terms of surrender, they found themselves being offered French wine and brandy and good food (the very last particles of food on the rock), with the invitation to partake freely, as they had a more than adequate stock. The government party were completely taken in by this ruse, and the Jacobites were allowed to withdraw with their arms and with the assurance that they might not be molested, but live at home in peace if they desired. For those who wanted to leave the country, a ship would be provided to take them to the Continent.

While this pressure against Jacobitism was being exerted on the political and military fronts, a similar pressure was being brought to bear on those responsible for higher education. In 1690, all schoolmasters teaching Latin were required to swear allegiance to King William and Queen Mary. The schoolmaster of North Berwick, "Mr Alexander Goodale" did so. But the post of schoolmaster was soon to change hands. By the following year, the schoolmaster was "Mr Walter Ainslie" and he was also precentor (leader of praise) and Session Clerk in the parish church.

There were changes, too, in the ministry and in the North Berwick Estate. In 1691, John Herbert, parish minister, died, and he was succeeded by Matthew Reid, who was ordained to the parish on 13th January 1692. Then, on 8th December 1694, The Honourable Sir Hew Dalrymple, Lord President of the Court of Session, third son of the first Lord Stair, the eminent Scots Jurist — a brother of John first Earl of Stair, sometime Secretary of State — took over the heritable debts of the confiscated estate of North Berwick and acquired the land, which his descendants have held to this day. In 1699 he purchased Tantallon Castle from the Douglases, and Leuchie from the Marjoribanks family in 1701. Later still, in 1706, he purchased the Bass Rock from the Crown.

With the coming of the Dalrymple family and with Matthew Reid settled as parish minister, the scene was now set for a new century in North Berwick, and a new chapter in this book.

THE EIGHTEENTH CENTURY — AND LATER

THE EIGHTEENTH CENTURY was only seven years old when the Union of the Parliaments of Scotland and England took place, an event which was regretted in some quarters, but in North Berwick was celebrated by the action of Sir Hew Dalrymple in planting trees on the east flank of the Law, and some on the north face. These are the trees which, now in their old age, are tall and gaunt, but in an earlier day were sturdy and bushy, and covered an area extending over much of the east and north sides of the hill. Sir Hew himself was one of the signatories of the Act of Union.

But before that event there were others of more local interest, preserved in the Diary of the Rev. George Turnbull, Minister of Tyninghame. On 20th December 1701 he records:

> "I was att Ann Hamilton Lady Sydserf her buriall. She died on Wednes. 17th by a fall off her horse, from behind her own son-in-law Mr Matthew reid minr att northberwicke"

A footnote explains that the deceased was wife of Robert Aitchison of Sydserf. Their daughter married Matthew Reid on 24th February 1693. Then there is an entry on 13th August 1702 which brings further bad news.

> "I was called to be with my neighbour Mr Matthew Reid minr att north berwicke when his wifs breast was to be cutt of a cancer for a second time; but the physicians thought fitt to delay it for some time, and take further adwice about it. they all agreed that her case was hopeless; the woman herself was pretty composed and shewed much Xan resolution; the physicans were Stewart, pitcarn younger, chirurgeons Eggar and Brown; all from Haddington. This was a most rainy day."

Turnbull's Diary contains yet one more entry of interest to North Berwick. On 7th May 1704, amongst other matters, he records:

"Mr Reid minr att North Berwick and I concurred to erect a school for the bairns of both our parochs at the haflen barns."

This school building at Halfland Barns is now occupied by a firm dealing in craft products, but as late as the 1890's it was still functioning as a primary day school under the chilly eye of the Scotch Education Department. Reports from that august body returning to the then parish minister of North Berwick, the Rev. G. W. Sprott, D.D., reveal that the building and facilities were hardly adequate at that time. The report of 1886, which unaccountably calls the school Halifax Barns Subscription School instead of Halfland Barns Subscription School, says:

". . . an easel for the blackboard is required. . . . The general efficiency of the school is very moderate. No systematic training in Intelligence seems to be given, and the grant under Article 19 (C) (1) could not be recommended."

The 1890 report says:

"The school has made good progress during the year. There is a tendency to talkativeness on the part of the younger children: otherwise the Discipline is excellent. The Junior section shows, on the whole, good results. Standard work is also generally good, with some weakness in the Spelling of the fourth Standard. Arithmetic is decidedly good. English is fair. The fourth — which includes about two-thirds of the older pupils — is weak in Intelligence and grammar, and Recitation is wanting in expression. Singing is very fair. Needlework is good. The lower part of the schoolroom walls is unsightly. It should be painted or (preferably) lined with wood."

Matthew Reid, having married into the landed gentry, had established himself in a commanding position when it came to the appointment of a successor. In fact, he became the founder of what one might describe as a dynasty of parish ministers of North Berwick. When he died, he was succeeded by his own son-in-law, George Murray, who had married Ann his daughter. Later in George Murray's life, North Berwick received a visit from the famous "Jupiter" Carlyle — to be precise, the Rev. Alexander Carlyle, later to become parish minister of Inveresk.

Paying a visit to the ministers in East Lothian, he describes in his autobiography what he thought of George Murray:

"The next clergyman, Mr George Murray of North Berwick, was in appearance quite the opposite of Mr Glen (the Minister of Dirleton), for he was a dry, withered stick, and as cold and repulsive in his manner as the other was kind and inviting; but he was not the less to be depended on **for that**, for he was very worthy and sensible, though, at the age of fifty, as torpid in mind as in body. His wife, however, of the name of Reid, the former minister's daughter, by whose interest he got the church, was as swift to speak as he was slow; and as he never interrupted her, she kept up the conversation, such as it was, without ceasing, except that her household affairs took her sometimes out of the room, when he began some metaphysical argument, but dropped it the moment she appeared, for he said Anny did not like these subjects. . . . Worn out, however, with the fatigue of the cherry feast (at Dirleton), I longed to be in bed, and took the first opportunity of a cessation in Anny's clapper to request to be shown to my room; this was complied with about eleven; but the worthy man accompanied me, and being at last safe and at liberty, he began a conversation on liberty and necessity, and the foundation of morals, and the Deistical controversy, that lasted till two in the morning."

George Murray and Ann Reid had a son Matthew who was destined for the ministry also; and in the course of time, Matthew succeeded George as Minister of North Berwick. Matthew married and had a son George, who also studied for the parish ministry with a view to succeeding his father. But at this point, tragedy struck. Matthew Murray died before his son George had completed his studies. Matthew's widow, however, was a woman of resource. She had a brother, the Rev. Professor Henry David Hill, of the chair of Greek at St Andrews University. He was called in to act as parish minister *pro tempore* until young George was ready for ordination. But Professor Hill was no mere "caretaker". As Minister of North Berwick, he was held in such esteem by the people of the town that he was made a Burgess of the Royal Burgh of North Berwick. George Murray II succeeded him, as expected, and his ministry lasted until his death in 1823. So Matthew Reid's dynasty had

North Berwick Pipe Band, 1901

F

In the 1880's — Quality Street, the Lodge, and a policeman

lasted for 131 years. At this point, it may be noted that it was Professor Hill who wrote the final version of the notes on the parish of North Berwick contained in the First Statistical Account of Scotland (1791), but acknowledges that they were based on notes written originally by Matthew Murray.

In this eighteenth century, in small communities like North Berwick, the Kirk, the Laird and the Town Council dominated the scene. The Dalrymple family, barons of North Berwick, resided in what is now known as the Lodge, but before 1783 was known as the Wall Tower. The origin of this name has nothing to do with a wall. Rather, it comes from the native pronunciation in the east of Scotland of the word "well". From boyhood holidays at a farm in Angus, the author remembers people who would refer to a well as a waal, or even in its diminutive form, as a waalie. In fact, any water supply, be it a pump, or domestic tap at the sink, might be referred to as a waal. The reference, then, in the case in point, is to the ancient St Andrew's Well lying close to the house near its south-west corner. The site of the Wall Tower, or Lodge is a preferential one, standing as it does at the head of the street in which, in this eighteenth century, the people of quality lived — hence the name Quality Street, though this had earlier been known as the Trongate. Centrally situated, at the junction of Quality Street and the High Street of the burgh, lay the Town Council chambers, with the jail on ground level and the council chamber proper above, reached by a stair in Quality Street. During this century, the clock tower which crowns the building had a straight-sided roof. The little Royal Burgh, ruled by its Council who jealously guarded its privileges, was surrounded by the lands of the Dalrymple family. But there was also the Suttie family who owned the Balgone estate. Turnbull's Diary, already referred to, mentions "Sir George Sowty of Begonn" in September 1699. At one period there was a Sir George Suttie who was M.P. for East Lothian. This family in 1818 added the word Grant, so becoming the Grant Sutties of Balgone.

Paul Sandby, R.A., who lived from 1725 to 1809 has left a sketch of the old church of North Berwick near the harbour as it was in his day. It shows the interior of two sides of the tower of the church, from which it can be deduced how the ringing chamber and the priest's room lay. On ground level, under a hemi-cylindrical roof of stone, a boat is to be seen. Doubtless the building it its state of disrepair was being used as a boathouse, while other members of the community would use the disjecta membra of the church to build their own houses. This drawing is somewhat earlier than another of some importance — the drawing by Col. Hutton — now in the National Library of Scotland. In the Hutton drawing, the point of observation is the sea wall at the harbour, and the view is towards the Law. There are no harbour buildings and no Forth Street. One looks right into the rear of the houses on the north side of High Street. Two sides of the tower of the harbour church remain standing. Beyond that, there is open country to the point where now the Information Centre stands. There, one sees a line of cottages forming a quarter-circle between Quality Street (the Trongate) and what is now Melbourne Place. The Town Chambers are there. Between the houses in High Street and the beach there seems to be an enclosed garden where Lorne Square now stands. There is a building on the site of Lauder's Hospital; and another on its left, formerly the house of the Dick family, now the Dalrymple Arms Hotel.

During the period of the Jacobite rising in 1745/46, the nearest North Berwick came to the scene of military action was when in 1745 the army of Prince Charles defeated the government troops under Sir John Cope at Prestonpans. But in the following year, after the Jacobites' defeat at Culloden, the "Gentleman's Magazine" dated April 1746, includes the following information:

"WHITEHALL, April 24 — This morning the Right Hon. The Lord Bury, Aide de camp to His Royal Highness the Duke of Cumberland arrived with a letter from His Royal Highness to His Majesty dated the 16th instant at Inverness; giving an account that His Royal Highness had that day obtained a complete victory over the rebels near Culloden House. Lord Bury was despatched on the 16th in the evening, immediately after His Royal Highness's arrival at Inverness, and came by sea from that place to North Berwick, where he landed on Monday last. The shortness of the time would not permit His Royal Highness to send any particulars of the action except that the rebel army was computed to amount to upwards of 8000 men; 1000 of which were left dead on the field of battle and about 600 taken prisoners. The Earl of Kilmarnock, Sir John Wedderburn, Mr Murray of Broughton, Secretary to the Pretender's son, the person stilled the French Amabssador and many others are taken prisoners. Lord Strathallan is said to be killed. All the rebels' cannon, and some colours, are taken.

His Royal Highness gives the greatest commendation of the behaviour of all the officers and soldiers under him.''

After the Jacobite war, Scotland once again became a place which might be visited without too much risk to life and limb. Bishop Pococke visited Scotland in 1760, and has left a description of the places he passed through, sending back regular letters to his sister. His passage on North Berwick is interesting, not only as an outsider's view of the town at that time, but also as an example of how even distinguished authors can be in serious error! He says:

"We came to that remarkable high Conical rock, called North Berwick Law, which I believe is wholly composed of Granite, of a bad red colour: We descended to North Berwick a small illbuilt town situated on a strand: A promontory stretches out from it which seems to have been an island, from the north end of which a pier is built that extends to the west, within which, vessels of 200 tons can come at spring tydes, but commonly those of about 100 tons;''

So far, so good — but then:

"On this promontory is a small ruined chapel arched over, and a tower a little to the north-west of it: They told me it was called St Elan and was a Monastery: I suppose it must have been the Cistertian nunnery built to the honour of the Virgin Mary in 1266 by Malcolm son of Duncan Earl of Fife.''

It wasn't the nunnery — it was the parish church — but it belonged to the nunnery. The dedication to "St Elan" is of course mistaken. Dr Richardson had the theory that the dear bishop had asked someone "What is that over there?" and had received the reply "That's the kirk-island" and had thought he had said "That's the Kirk-Elan". Finally, the nunnery was built not in 1266 but before 1154.

61

The bishop continues:

"This town has a trade from their distilleries and Manufacture of starch: They also have large granaries here, and export a great quantity of malt and several kind of grain".

There were no large granaries in North Berwick in 1760, and no distillery nor place for the manufacture of starch was otherwise known. But Berwick-on-Tweed had these things. He was not the last person to confuse North Berwick with Berwick-on-Tweed. The letter from which this is quoted was sent from Berwick-on-Tweed. Yet he was still thinking of a town north of the border, for he continues:

"It is said that King Edward 1st after the Battle of Banock Burne gave up this Castle and retired to the Castle of Dunbar."

Passing over the fact that it was not Edward I but Edward II who was defeated at Bannockburn, it is difficult to know to what castle he is referring. North Berwick's only "Castle" is the Castle Hill, and this is purely a prehistoric construction. It cannot be Tantallon, because he immediately goes on:

"I proceeded two miles to Tantallon Castle at the mouth of the great bay, called the Firth of Forth . . . etc."

About this time, a man from North Berwick, William Anderson, went out with Captain Cook in his ship, *H.M. Sloop Resolution,* on his famous voyage of discovery in the Pacific Ocean. He went as ship's surgeon and was later employed by Capt. Cook as naturalist. Sadly, he did not complete the voyage, dying on board ship before it returned home, after the murder of Capt. Cook.

His father, Robert Anderson, was schoolmaster at North Berwick Grammar School, which stood on the site now occupied by Victoria House, at the junction of High Street and Market Place. William Anderson's aunt and uncle lived at the Mains farmhouse. Robert Anderson retired in 1756 and went elsewhere to better his circumstances, but before he departed, he was made a burgess of the Royal Burgh of North Berwick.

In 1789, North Berwick had another visitor — this time James Haldane, a member of a family who spent much time campaigning for a form of church government which stressed the independence of the congregation from any pressure from prelates or superior courts of the church. In his biography, it is described how James Haldane started preaching on the beach at North Berwick. He had gathered a crowd, when word of his arrival was taken to the Town Council, who happened to be in session at the time. This was a violation of the Council's authority, according to the thinking of the time, and the councillors came down in a body to expel him from their property. They had been, says Haldane's biographer, in their cups, and told him in no uncertain manner to clear off. Haldane, however, retaliated by pointing out that he was below the high-water mark, and they had no law whereby they could remove him, as their burgh stopped at the high-water mark. They replied that if they had no law, they would soon make one. At this, a farmer in the crowd said that he would put a field at the preacher's disposal, and the whole assembly moved away to the new location. But the Town Council was not to be outdone. The Town Drummer was instructed to walk up and down the road as near to the preacher as possible, to drown his words!

Two years later, the First Statistical Account of Scotland tells of North Berwick that the town's population was about 700, and that throughout the countryside the enclosing of fields was continuing, and that soon there would be no land which had not been enclosed. Also, there was now a stage coach which ran between Edinburgh and North Berwick.

At the time of the Napoleonic Wars, North Berwick made its contribution to the defence of the nation. An observation post was set up on the Law, near its summit, so that a watch could be kept for French vessels. This is now seen as the ruined cottage familiar to all who climb the Law, or see it daily from their own homes. The Law's usefulness as a lookout point was proved over 100 years later when, at the time of the First World War, a second observation post was constructed, this time with a concrete roof.

By 1797 North Berwick had raised a corps of Volunteers. In a Muster Roll of 1801, they numbered three commissioned officers including their commander Captain Robert Burn, eight N.C.O's and 52 privates. Much later, in December 1859, the inhabitants of North Berwick and neighbourhood, under the chairmanship of Sir Hew Dalrymple, the sixth baronet, resolved to raise a Volunteer Artillery Corps. Two months later, in

February 1860, Queen Victoria accepted the offer of the services of a Company of Artillery Volunteers at North Berwick.

The harbour was also brought up to date, by being deepened in 1804, and the harbour walls so modified to make "the south pier . . . level betwixt the cross pier and the present south, with one stone paul and a cart road down the east end in to the harbour". This was done at a cost of £102 3s. 4d.

With the defeat of Napoleon at Waterloo in 1815 and the coming of peace, Britain found herself in a position of favour and leadership in Europe, and the church in North Berwick found itself able to afford a new Manse which was built in 1825 in a style reminiscent of the Adam brothers, and which reflected the social position of the minister. The Murray "dynasty" had now died out and the new minister was the Rev. Robert Balfour Graham, who had a son Henry Grey Graham, the author of the famous work "The Social Life of Scotland in the Eighteenth Century", who was also known for his very strong anti-Presbyterian views.

In the early 1830's there arrived in North Berwick a number of fishing families from Fife. It is to this immigration that the Millars, the Fosters and the Kellys trace their descent. Coincident with this influx, the buildings at the harbour, characterised by their warm red colour, were built. In these, a hardy race of North Berwick fishing families was raised. Accommodation and facilities might be at a minimum, and the east wind might blow through the premises from time to time snell and keen, but these families grew and prospered as part of the life of the town. Use was also made of these red buildings for storage purposes, for goods for import or export, grain for export, guano imported from the Bass Rock.

An oil painting dated 1836 shows a Dutch coaster at anchor in the East Bay, said to be taking water from a spring which surfaced near where the present Coastguard cottages stand. It also shows North Berwick covered in a light blue haze, the smoke from so many coal fires in the town, drifting gently from west to east.

To this same year also belongs a list of "Heads of families who are, and have been resident in the parish of North Berwick for a space of one year preceding this date — 5th December 1836 and are in full communion with the church". This list contains the names of 80 heads of families resident in the Burgh of North Berwick, and 98 names of heads of families lying within the parish but outside the Burgh. All the familiar names of the farms are there, plus the now unused names of Sowhole and Mary Place.

About 1900—The lifeboat Fergus Ferguson *at home*

"THE BIARRITZ OF THE NORTH"

THE COMING of railway transport was, throughout the entire country, a factor of the greatest possible importance for social change of every sort. Reference need only be made to general histories of the nineteenth century to see how far-reaching these social changes were. Between the coming of railway services in the first half of that century and the scene 50 years later there is a world of difference.

In North Berwick, the change, when it came, was equally profound, if comparison is made between the North Berwick of pre-railway days and the North Berwick of, say, the year 1900.

Planning of the railway began some time in the late 1840's. According to the late Dr J. S. Richardson, one of the earliest ideas was that the railway should come right into the town, following the line, roughly, of Forth Street, and curving round with the West Bay until it reached the harbour. A causeway was then to be built from the Platcock Rocks out to sea to join up with the Craig. On this causeway there was to be the railway, and the new deep-water anchorage for shipping thus formed would make North Berwick into a major Scottish port able to deal with bulk freight of any sort, like, for example, Leith. The gasworks was located on the site of the old church at the harbour (all memory of its function as North Berwick's Parish Church for about 500 years had long vanished). This plan however was dropped, and the railway was not permitted to extend further than the present railway station, except that coal wagons were permitted to come on to the embankment which is at present within the Royal Hotel grounds, and unload their coal over the north side of that embankment to feed the gasworks when it was moved to that position in 1860, on the site now occupied by the Bass Rock Garage, and the shops on Station Hill. The placing of the passenger railway station where it now is had one other consequence — it meant that the terminus was at the foot of a downward incline, and in frosty weather when adhesion to the rail was uncertain, incoming trains ran the risk of being unable to stop, and crashing into the buffers. There

About 1900—The Fergus Ferguson *is launched*

Queen Victoria Diamond Jubilee Procession
F (North Berwick) Company, 7th Volunteer Battalion, Royal Scots Fusiliers
Lieut. Frank Crombie
Surgeon Col. J. L. Crombie

have been a number of occasions when trains have done this. One was on 20th August 1904. Other similar accidents have occurred from time to time in more recent years.

But this was all in the future in the 1840's. North Berwick was still a quiet little town, yet conscious of its connections with the Scottish nobility, and conscious, too, that it was able to provide excellent facilities for that up-and-coming sport for gentlemen, and all others who cared to follow them in this pursuit — golf. Sir Francis Grant's painting of "Golf at North Berwick", dating from the 1840's, shows the leisured ease associated with the game at that time — gentlemen in top hats, one on horseback, picnic hampers with wine bottles, all close to where a player is "holing out". Sir Hew Hamilton-Dalrymple, the tenth baronet, has captured the feeling of these early days of golf in North Berwick when he writes:

> "In the early days the members of North Berwick Golf Club consisted of the county families and their friends. For them, no accommodation was then provided in the town. Each country house within a driving radius had its contingent of visitors who generally arrived on the scene a day or two before the meeting of the Club. On the morning of the meeting, parties drove down in great style to North Berwick and for their accommodation a tent was erected on the green in proximity to the first teeing ground."

The town of North Berwick itself at this time is described in an article in *The Scotsman* of 9th October 1902, in the following terms: "When Albert Edward Prince of Wales paid his visit to the town on the 20th August 1859 it was little more than a fishing village of two streets — the thoroughfares still known as High Street and Quality Street. The latter was so-called because in it were the houses of a number of well-to-do persons — scions of county families and retired naval and military officers. The streets were unpaved; the water supply was obtained from street wells; the drainage system consisted of the open gutter. The postmaster found one small boy sufficient to aid him in the discharge of his duties. Even then, however, some had found out the invigorating qualities of North Berwick air . . . the beach on both sides of the harbour presents fine gently-sloping sands and forms excellent bathing-ground; the links afford good scope for the healthy diversion of golfing; and the firth, the rocky isles, the low trap hills to landward, and especially North Berwick

Law, immediately south of the town, with a rich skirt of wood and a delightful zig-zag walk to the summit, comprise enough of scenery to give very pleasing exercise to the imagination. The result is that North Berwick is a select place — attracting a larger proportion of wealthy and well-informed visitors than most towns of its size.''

The Scotsman's interest in North Berwick of old, in 1902, is explained by the second visit paid by the same royal personage, now King Edward VII, in 1902.

The railway arrived in North Berwick in 1850. A single line had been laid, though space was left for adding a second line should traffic justify this. But results were disappointing at first, and in 1856 the service between North Berwick and Drem was reduced from a steam train to a horse-drawn rail coach. But North Berwick was beginning to grow, and the traffic of summer visitors was increasing, especially as golf was becoming more and more popular in the second half of the century. To attempt to capitalise on the golf traffic still further, a second railway line was projected, taking off from the main line at Spittal, to the east of Longniddry, and connecting up Aberlady, Gullane, and North Berwick. But though this line reached Gullane by 1898, the gap between Gullane and North Berwick was never bridged by rail, and the Aberlady, Gullane and North Berwick Railway Company was taken over by the North British in 1890.

In 1859, as already quoted, the Prince of Wales visited North Berwick, arriving by rail. The town, from the station to Quality Street, was garlanded with flowers for the occasion. Three triumphal arches composed of flowers and evergreens had been erected, with flags surmounting them, bearing appropriate words of welcome. From most of the windows, flags and banners were hung. The entrance gates and lodge of Sir Hew Dalrymple's mansion were decorated with flowers in wreaths and festoons. The fishing craft in the harbour flew flags at the masthead, and on the Law the royal flag was displayed. The magistrates of the Royal Burgh in their official capacity, headed by Mr James Dall, the Chief Magistrate (they were uncertain whether the word Provost could be rightly used), welcomed the Prince. Along with his suite, the Prince embarked on Sir Hew Dalrymple's yacht *Firefly* at Canty Bay which, accompanied by H.M. gunboat *Louisa,* made for the Bass. There the Prince enjoyed some shooting, and brought down a number of gannets. Later, he

A topsail schooner in North Berwick harbour last century

Dirleton Avenue before 1888

On left, garden wall of Bramerton, on right, entrance to Ware Road (north)

visited Tantallon Castle and Archerfield, and on the Sunday, attended divine service in Dirleton Church.

But the future King Edward VII was not the only royal visitor to North Berwick. On 29th September 1860, the Duchess of Kent, the mother of Queen Victoria, visited North Berwick, shortly before her death, while she was on a visit to Archerfield. Then there was Arthur, Duke of Connaught, who was in Edinburgh with his regiment, and passed through the burgh in 1876 on his way to Tantallon Castle. Queen Victoria herself visited Tantallon Castle (though not North Berwick) in 1878, and there were visits of the Duke of Edinburgh (afterwards Duke of Saxe-Coburg Gotha).

By the late 1850's and early 1860's North Berwick was expanding. A print showing a picnic on the Craig, with the whole town of North Berwick displayed in the background, dated 1861, shows that North Berwick had begun expanding eastwards. While there was still an iron foundry at the foot of Balfour Street, the houses in the Quadrant had been built, and there were isolated large houses in what is now North Berwick's west end. Robert Louis Stevenson was to live for a short time in one of the Quadrant houses.

The major development of North Berwick, however, which was just starting to take place at this time, was to the west of the town, where, over the next 50 years, many fine houses were to be built.

Many of the new residents in this expanding North Berwick belonged to the cream of London society, and were accustomed, amongst other things, to attend church on a Sunday where the service would be conducted according to the Anglican pattern. To cater for their needs, a church of the Episcopal Church of Scotland was erected, at the eastern end of Dirleton Avenue, and consecrated by the Bishop of Oxford in 1863, dedicated in honour of St Baldred, the eighth-century pioneer mentioned in the first chapter of this book. This church is served by a Rector. The first rector, the Rev. F. L. M. Anderson, had as his rectory the house now known as Minto House, in York Road, and it is said that he kept there an ambitious establishment, and went hunting and shooting with the gentry.

Five years later, in 1868, the foundation stone of what is now Abbey Church was laid, to house the United Presbyterian congregation. The United Presbyterian Church of Scotland took its descent from the Secession from the Church of Scotland by Ebenezer Erskine and his followers in 1733 to form the Associate Synod. After a complicated history of division and recombination, this body formed the United Secession Church which in 1847 united with the church of the Relief Synod to form the United Presbyterian Church of Scotland.

In North Berwick, the Associate congregation first met for worship in a "meeting house" built in 1778 on the site of William Auld & Son's (now Thomson's) premises in the Westgate. In 1782 they were officially recognised as the United Associate congregation for the town and in due course in 1847 became the United Presbyterian Church. Their 1868 church building was originally known as the United Presbyterian Church of the Martyrs. Then, in 1900, throughout Scotland there was a union between the Free Church and the United Presbyterian Church to form the United Free Church of Scotland. As from this date, the North Berwick U.P. Church took the name Abbey Church, as the ground on which it was built originally belonged to the Abbey. To complete the story, in 1929 the United Free Church of Scotland and the Church of Scotland were united, thus recombining in one many of the historic strands of Scottish church life. As from this date, Abbey Church, Blackadder Church (formerly Free Church) and St Andrew's (parish church of old) became sister parish churches within the Church of Scotland.

To cater for the needs of the Roman Catholics living in and around North Berwick — some of them farm workers of Irish descent, some of them residents in the town — ground for the building of a church was obtained from Sir Hew Dalrymple. The foundation stone was laid in May 1879, and the future building dedicated in the name of Our Lady, Star of the Sea. Later that same year, on 24th September, the nave of the church was ready for use as a place of worship, and was blessed by Archbishop Strain. It was not, however, until the same date in the year 1930 that the entire church was officially consecrated, being now complete and free of debt. This service was conducted by the Archbishop of St Andrews and Edinburgh, Archbishop Macdonald.

Meantime, the Parish Church was beginning to feel outclassed by these new church buildings. It had served the parish for about 200 years. It was dark and inclined to be damp. It had

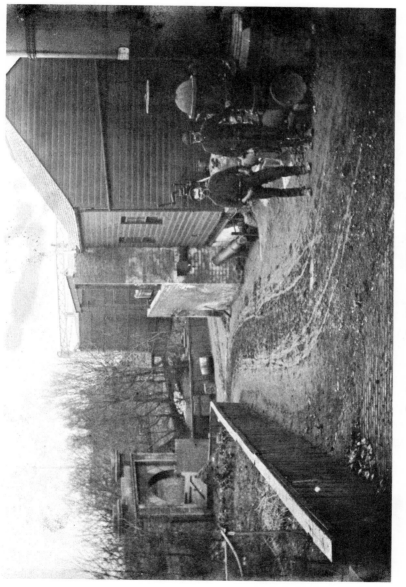

In the gasworks (Station Hill) (1860-1904)

Post Office and postal staff, about 1903. These premises are now in use by J. Coventry & Son

none of the grace of St Baldred's nor the spaciousness of the United Presbyterian Church. Something had to be done. First, a plan was brought forward for enlarging the church building. But this raised a storm of protest. The building would then rest on the dead of the parish! Nothing but a new church would suffice. The heritors acceded to this.

In 1874, the Rev. George Washington Sprott had been inducted. He brought with him a fresh outlook on church affairs in the town. He was much influenced by the liturgical movement within the church, and was a founder member of the Church Service Society. For this he was known throughout the church. Yet his local reputation rested on more than this. A faithful visitor of his parish, it was in his time that the Guild of St Margaret was instituted, an organisation for the women of the church, out of which, along with similar bodies in other parishes, the Woman's Guild of the Church of Scotland was born.

Dr Sprott's legacy to North Berwick in the 1870's and 80's must lie in the direction he sought to give to the work of building the new parish church. The site of the former Manse in High Street prior to 1825 was available, so it was here that, in 1882, Sir Hew Dalrymple, the sixth baronet, laid the foundation stone of the new church, designed by Sir Rowand Anderson, and built in Gothic Revival style. It was complete and ready for use in June 1883 — but without the tower and the hall. These were later additions — the hall in 1901 and the tower in 1907.

The development of the western part of North Berwick proceeded apace during the later years of last century. Under the lairds of North Berwick, and in particular under Sir Walter Dalrymple, the eighth baronet, the land on either side of Dirleton Avenue, starting with land formerly belonging to the Abbey farm, was feued for house building, and this process continued up to the beginning of the First World War. It resulted in a development which has always been considered one of the best of this period. These houses were inhabited, many on a summer-only basis, by figures from London Society. The division of these houses into flats is a mid-twentieth-century development. Indeed, when during the early years of this century, North Berwick was publicised as "the Biarritz of the North"; there was solid evidence for this claim. It was fashionable society's choice as a golfing and holiday resort. One of the key figures in North Berwick at this time was Ben Sayers.

Bernard Sayers, a small man of 5 ft. 3 ins. weighing under 10 stones (140 lbs.), was born at Leith in 1857. At the age of 16 he took up golf, receiving his early lessons from James Kaye, professional at Seaton Carew. By 1873 he was teaching golf at North Berwick and making a name for himself as an expert in the game, with gifts of agility and humour. Later, he could number Grand Duke Michael of Russia, Prince Edward of Saxe-Weimar, Queen Alexandra and the Duke of Connaught among his pupils. Ben Sayers was one of the pioneers of a new regime in which the professional player acquired a new and respected social status. He was an admirable putter, and a shrewd observer of golf and golfers.

At the same time, he was one of the early manufacturers of gutta-percha golf balls. His son, George Sayers, who held an American professional post at Merion Club, Philadelphia, recalls how this process started as a kitchen-based family enterprise. Pieces of gutta-percha of the required weight — 26½ to 28 penny-weights — were dropped into boiling water to soften. Then they were worked or squeezed by hand to expel any bubbles. Each piece was then placed in a brass mould, pressed, and then tossed into a tub of cold water to harden. At the end of the day, the balls were placed in a frame to dry. Twelve dozen balls a day were turned out by this method. The next day the balls received the first of their four to six coats of paint, but, to create the irregular surface necessary for a true-flying ball, they were first hammered. Later, they were at this stage cut by a machine, and, later still, moulded with nicks or cuts. These "gutty" balls were stored for many months to be seasoned. This type of ball was used until 1901 when it was superseded by the rubber-cored ball, whose basic design is that still in use.

Though Ben Sayers never won the Open Championship, he was runner-up in 1888, third in 1889, and sixth in 1896. He represented Scotland against England each year from 1903 to 1913, except in 1911, and in 1908, when the match was cancelled because of bad weather.

His partnership with Andrew Kirkaldy in foursomes competition play made a well-nigh unbeatable combination, with success following success. The only defeat suffered by Sayers and

Ben Sayers, 1857-1924

View from Platcock Rocks before the swimming pool was constructed

Kirkcaldy was at St Andrews in 1910, when they were beaten 2 and 1 by Robson and Renouf.

Early in this century Ben Sayers became the first golf professional at Monte Carlo. He also toured America in 1914 and 1915 and played on one occasion with President Taft. His clubmaking business in North Berwick expanded and he began supplying clubs all over the world.

Ben Sayers died at 115 High Street, North Berwick, in March 1924, aged 67. Notable among the wreaths at his funeral was one in the joint names of Sandy Herd, Harry Vardon, J. H. Taylor and James Braid. He is also remembered locally as a head of a family with which many other professional golfers from North Berwick could claim connection by blood or by marriage. David Grant was his cousin, and Arthur Grant who was professional at Le Touquet until after World War II, was David Grant's son. Norman Grant, another son of David Grant, was personal golf professional to the Aga Khan at Cannes for many years, while Jack White was a relation through marriage. Arthur Fennell's mother was Kitty Grant, a sister of Arthur, Norman and Ben Grant.

Golf, however, was not the only sporting interest in North Berwick at this time. In the 1880's there was an annual horse race to the top of the Law and back again. The author is indebted to Alexr. Struth for the following information about one of the competitors, a horse called Umpire, whose sire had been an Arab stallion, and who had inherited tremendous stamina. According to family tradition, this horse was winner of the Law race four years in succession. Many of the county families wanted to buy Umpire, but the owner would never sell. On one occasion, for a wager, Umpire took his master from North Berwick to Linlithgow, a journey of over 40 miles, took part in a point-to-point race there, and returned with his master to North Berwick the following day. When war broke out in 1914 and his master enlisted, Umpire, now a veteran of 33 years of age, had to be "put to sleep" as there was now no one to look after him; and he was buried in the Glebe along with two other horses. To bring the story up to date, recent (1980) excavations on the lower part of the Glebe, now converted into a car park by the District Council, have not unearthed any equine remains!

During the last decade of the nineteenth century, North Berwick received a different kind of visitor — The Rev. Jacob

Primmer. He paid an annual visit to the old kirk at the harbour where he would hold an open-air service. Apprenticed as a printer, he had become a minister of the Church of Scotland, and was ordained to Townhead Church, Dunfermline, in 1878, from which he resigned in 1904. He died in 1914. He is remembered particularly for his strong anti-Roman Catholic views, and his pamphleteering against those who might seem to adopt any "high church" views. His many publications include "The Scottish Hymnal saturated with Popish error, Superstition and Idolatry" (1891), and, in the same year, "The Secret Traitorous Romanising Church Service Society". His annual presence in North Berwick may be put down to the fact that, as already indicated, the parish minister, Dr G. W. Sprott was a founder member of this Society. A photograph of the Rev. Jacob Primmer speaking to a number of fishermen near the harbour shows him as a man of middle height with a beard, wearing a flat black hat and a dark overcoat.

By the turn of the century, sea bathing was regulated. In 1901, a local information card gives the information:

> "Gentlemen can bathe from any part of the beach until 8 a.m., after that from West of the Marine Dyke or East of Tantallon Terrace".

while the same card gives the train service between Edinburgh and North Berwick at that period:

N. Berwick leave	Edinburgh arrive	Edinburgh leave	N. Berwick arrive
7.10 a.m.	8.24 a.m.	6.55 a.m.	8.03 a.m.
8.50 a.m.	9.34 a.m.	9.17 a.m.	10.20 a.m.
11.10 a.m.	12.18 p.m.	10.20 a.m.	11.02 a.m.
1.45 p.m.	2.45 p.m.	*1.40 p.m.	2.25 p.m.
4.15 p.m.	5.19 p.m.	1.45 p.m.	2.43 p.m.
a6.45 p.m.	8.00 p.m.	4.35 p.m.	5.26 p.m.
*6.45 p.m.	7.43 p.m.	5.15 p.m.	6.16 p.m.
*9.15 p.m.	10.10 p.m.	6.30 p.m.	7.30 p.m.
		8.15 p.m.	9.10 p.m.
		10.25 p.m.	11.07 p.m.

*—Saturdays only   a—Except Saturdays

FARES — North Berwick to Edinburgh — 1st, 3s. 6d; 3rd, 1s. 10½d. Return — 1st, 5s. 6d; 3rd, 3s. 9d. Saturday Fares— Edinburgh to North Berwick and North Berwick to

NOT TRANSFERABLE.   *10.*

VISIT OF HIS MAJESTY KING EDWARD VII.
TO NORTH BERWICK

ADMIT THE BEARER

Mr D. B Swan,

Town Clerk Depute

to the Railway Station on the occasion of the
King's arrival on 9th and on his departure on
11th October 1902.

Entrance by North Door half-an-hour before His Majesty's
arrival and departure.

MORNING DRESS.

A. D. WALLACE, *Town Clerk*.

Train at North Berwick Station in the 1920's

Edinburgh, available day of issue only — Return, 1st, 3s. 6d; 3rd, 2s. 1d. Available till Monday — North Berwick to Edinburgh and Edinburgh to North Berwick — Return, 1st, 4s. 1d; 3rd 2s. 4d. Friday to Monday Tickets, both ways — 1st, 4s. 1d.; 3rd, 2s. 4d.

FORTNIGHTLY TICKETS TO NORTH BERWICK — From Edinburgh (Waverley) to North Berwick — 1st Class, £1 12s.; 3rd Class, £1 5s. Through carriages are run from North Berwick to Edinburgh by all trains except 7.10 a.m. and 1.45 p.m.

About the turn of the century, North Berwick had a number of festival occasions, organised by the Royal Burgh to celebrate events of importance. Queen Victoria's Diamond Jubilee, for example, was celebrated with a banquet in the Foresters' Hall (now the Playhouse Cinema) on 22nd June 1897, at which Grace was said by the Rev. Dr Sprott, and the loyal toast proposed by Sir Walter H. Dalrymple, Bt. The toast "The Prince and Princess of Wales and other members of the Royal Family" was proposed by Provost Brodie. There was a band to play the National Anthem and "Rule Britannia", and two singers. The toast "Army, Navy and Reserve Forces" was proposed by Mr T. S. Glover, Rector of North Berwick High School, to which the reply was made by Lieut.-Col. Guild.

The entry of British troops into Pretoria was marked on 6th June 1900 by rejoicings which started at 4 p.m. with a procession which included every official and unofficial body, leaving the Council Chambers and going along High Street, Dirleton Avenue, Hamilton Road, York Road, Links Road, West Bay, Beach Road, Forth Street, Melbourne Place, Quadrant and East Road back to the starting point. Then the National Anthem was sung, and the Volunteers fired a feu de joie. From 7 to 8 p.m. the band played a selection of tunes on the West Links. Then at 9.15 the town was "illuminated", and at 9.30 there was a torchlight procession from the Council Chambers. At 10.15 there was a firework display on the West Links, and a bonfire at 10.30. Finally, all joined in singing "Rule Britannia". A collection on behalf of *The Scotsman* Shilling fund for soldiers' widows and orphans was taken at the procession.

When Queen Victoria died in 1901, there was a procession from the Council chambers to St Andrew's Church for a memorial service. Some time later, Provost John Macintyre and two of the Bailies, James Glass and Thomas Himsworth, erected a circular stained glass window in this church in memory of the late Queen. It contains the national emblems of the component parts of Great Britain — England, Scotland and Ireland; and the Burgh's coat of arms is in the centre.

To mark King Edward VII's Coronation in 1902, it was first planned to have civic celebrations in June of that year, but these were postponed to Friday and Saturday the 8th and 9th of August. On the Friday there was a Handicap Golf Competition for Amateurs and Caddies, starting at 4 p.m. At 7 p.m. there was a Children's Character Fancy Dress Ball in the Foresters' Hall, and at 9.30 an Adults' Dance in the Foresters' Hall (double ticket four shillings). On the Saturday at 9.30 a.m., Coronation mugs and medals were presented to the school children in the Public School (in School Road). Then at noon, a grand procession, and at 1 p.m. a combined religious service on the East Links. At 2.45 "aquatic sports" in the swimming pond, followed at 4.30 by a Yacht Race, at 6 p.m. a Bowling Tournament on North Berwick Bowling Green, at 8.45 the illumination of the town, and at 9 p.m. a Lantern Procession, covering the same route as the earlier one. In the procession were all the local dignitaries, along with the following bodies — Brass Band, Coastguards, Yeomanry, Volunteers, Cadet Corps, Freemasons, Oddfellows, Lifeboat Crew, Foresters, Rocket Brigade, Good Templars, Fire Brigade, Pipe Band, School Children, Post Office Officials, and Boys' Institute. The Rocket Brigade, whose photograph is in the local Museum, used the south porch of the old church at the harbour to house their apparatus.

In October 1902 King Edward VII paid a short visit to North Berwick while on his way south from Balmoral Castle. Preparations for his visit were worthy of a state occasion, although the King had specially requested that there be no speeches, no bouquets, and no guard of honour. He was due to arrive by rail on 9th October and depart again by train on 11th October. On both these occasions, admission to the railway station was by the Town Council's invitation only; entrance was by the north door "half an hour before His Majesty's arrival and departure"; and morning dress was to be worn. Children were given a holiday from school to see the king arrive.

KING EDWARD'S HOST AND HOSTESS

The Prince and Princess of Saxe-Weimar, who have been entertaining the King at North Berwick

From the Edinburgh Evening Dispatch, 11th October 1902

H.M. The King at North Berwick

King Edward VII plants a tree near the steps of the Council Chambers, 10th October 1902

The King stayed with his relations Prince and Princess Edward of Saxe Weimar, at the Knoll, a house in Clifford Road which at that time was the property of a Dr G. A. Berry, an Edinburgh ophthalmic surgeon. To commemorate this short visit the house was renamed *King's Knoll* after the King's departure. Today it bears this name as a holiday home under the British Red Cross Society. The King's host, who had earlier distinguished himself as a soldier in the Crimean War, held the title Field Marshal His Highness Prince Edward of Saxe Weimar, K.P., G.C.B., G.C.V.O. Later that same month, on 25th October, he was given the freedom of the Burgh of North Berwick at a ceremony in the Foresters' Hall.

Ostensibly the King was in North Berwick to recover from his appendicitis operation, but his programme was a crowded one.

At 3 p.m. on 10th October, King Edward planted a sycamore tree near the foot of the steps leading to the Council Chambers. The Town Council were ready with a heavy wooden protective guard to place in position immediately after the planting, so that the tree might be unharmed by vandals or souvenir-hunters. Provost McIntyre presented the King with a silver spade to mark the occasion. Later, the King visited Tyninghame House, the seat of the Earl of Haddington, to plant a tree on the west side of the mansionhouse, and it was also planned to pay a visit to Whittinghame to see The Rt. Hon. A. J. Balfour, who at that time was Prime Minister. That evening at 6.15 p.m. the King attended the Town Illuminations. Next day, he departed by train at 10 a.m.

Aside from the affairs of the King and the nobility, the lot of the average mortal in North Berwick had been improving, thanks largely to a very active Provost and Town Council. A new water supply to the town had been instituted. There was now a new infectious diseases hospital at Gilsland, a new slaughterhouse and a new cemetery in Dunbar Road. But the most striking of the new developments in the eyes of holidaymakers was the building of the swimming pool in a previously unsalubrious hole in the rocks at the harbour, along with a wide open esplanade. This was to be the site, later, of an open-air stage for entertainers, while the swimming pool was used for galas and for the physical recreation and training of the young people of North Berwick in swimming and diving.

The gasworks had had a varied career. Starting on the site of the old kirk at the harbour, it had been moved first to the west links, to a point on what is at present the eighteenth fairway, approximately opposite Point Garry Hotel. Then in 1860, it was moved to the site of the present Bass Rock Garage. Now, in 1904, it was again moved, this time to its present location beyond Williamston. If the progress of North Berwick can be measured in gas, the following data may be of interest. In 1893 between 8 and 9 million cubic feet of gas were made and used. By 1903/4, this figure had risen to over 23 million. In 1894-95, 1,149 tons of coal were carbonised; in 1903/4, the figure was 2,474 tons. According to the report in the *Haddingtonshire Courier* of 14th October 1904, "The construction of the works began last autumn, under the supervision of the engineer, Mr James McGilchrist, gas engineer, Dumbarton, a gentleman of wide experience in his profession".

Mention has been made of the Rocket life-saving apparatus and the body of men who manned it. North Berwick had also a lifeboat. From 1887 to 1902 it was the *Fergus Ferguson,* a rowing boat powered by over a dozen sturdy oarsmen. It was housed in what is now the Victoria Cafe, but was then the lifeboat house. The doorway was in Victoria Road, and the boat, on its heavy wheeled cradle would sit facing across the street towards the top of the slipway. This is nowadays closed by a wooden partition. On festive occasions the lifeboat on its cradle would be taken in procession round the town, pulled by two strong farm horses. "Lifeboat Day" when funds were raised for the cause of the saving of life at sea, has always been a feature of North Berwick.

To this halcyon age also belong the pleasure steamers which called at North Berwick. These paddle steamers were run by Galloways of Leith, and an old gentleman known to the author who knew this company well recalls that these steamers were the personal hobby of Mr Galloway. He knew that they didn't make money, but so long as they didn't lose too much, he was quite happy. They plied from Leith over to Elie, then back across the firth again to North Berwick, and if the weather was good and there were enough passengers, they might go to the Isle of May, then return the way they had come. They were never quite so popular with visitors as, say, the Clyde steamers were with the people of the west of Scotland, when they went "doon the watter". Often, it is said, visitors would be seasick on the rough

Galloway's paddle steamer, Redgauntlet near the jetty

The Tantallon Castle, *at North Berwick*

leg of the voyage, between Elie and North Berwick, and would opt to go back to Edinburgh by train rather than face the return journey by boat. Photographs of two of the Galloway steamers are in the possession of North Berwick Environment Trust — the single-funnelled *Redgauntlet* and the twin-funnelled *Tantallon Castle*. The pier used by the steamers consisted of the foundations which are still in existence, just to the west of the swimming pool, and on top of them, a superstructure which has now been substantially removed. This gave access on three levels, thus allowing for different states of the tide. With the advent of war in 1914, however, the whole enterprise was abandoned, and North Berwick never saw the Galloway steamers again.

As the visitors flocked to North Berwick, the demand on the golf course increased. In 1893 Sir Walter Dalrymple, the eighth baronet, and a number of other gentlemen took steps to lay out a nine-hole course on the ground between the Rhodes Farm and the sea. The new course was opened on 16th April 1894 by Sir Walter driving off the first ball before a large and fashionable company. Twelve years later, the Town Council bought land from Sir Walter, 129 acres, part of Rhodes and Castleton farms, extending the original nine-hole course into a full 18-hole course, equal in length to the west course. It was laid out by James Braid, the Open Champion, and Ben Sayers, who at that time was the local professional. The Town Council even managed to arrange a concessionary fare on the railway between North Berwick and Edinburgh for the members of "the North Berwick Corporation Golf Clubs", first class return being 3/6 and third class return 2/5.

In 1904 a North Berwick man, Jack White, who had been golf professional at Sunningdale for 25 years, won the British Open Championship at Sandwich with a score of 297. He was the only man from East Lothian ever to win this honour, and the first man in the history of the championship to break 300. He was a member of a North Berwick family who made their mark on world-wide competitive golf. Wilfred Thomson was his brother-in-law and Jimmy Thomson his nephew (see later chapter).

Having been visited by royalty and the nobility and having entertained them to their satisfaction, North Berwick also achieved the distinction of having the Prime Minister of Great

Britain, the Rt. Hon. A. J. Balfour, opening a Sale of Work in the Foresters' Hall some time between 1902 and 1904. Nothing but the best was good enough for North Berwick!

The coming of war in 1914, which, throughout the country brought about such changes in social and economic order, dampened, but did not extinguish, the glory of North Berwick. It was said, half in jest and half in earnest, that if the Zeppelins bombed London, the seat of government of this country could be moved from London to North Berwick without too much difficulty, as there were so many in high positions who had houses in North Berwick. But this was a fate which did not befall North Berwick.

RECENT TIMES — 1914-1939

WITH THE outbreak of war in 1914 North Berwick, like every other community, adapted itself to wartime conditions. A batallion of Royal Scots was stationed in the area, and there resulted, as might be expected, many marriages between the troops and the eligible local young ladies! The recently-constructed Parish Church Hall was pressed into service as a Canteen for the Forces, under the leadership of Mrs J. B. Whitelaw, daughter-in-law of Sir William Whitelaw, Chairman of the London and North Eastern Railway Company.

North Berwick lost 154 men during the 1914-18 war.

In August 1916, East Fortune airfield was taken over by the government for the Royal Naval Air Service. As from that time, it was associated with the development of airships. The climax of this work came in the summer of 1919. The R34, a rigid airship, was delivered to East Fortune from Beardmores of Inchinnan in May that year. In the early hours of 2nd July she left East Fortune "with a crew of 30, a stowaway and a kitten". She crossed the Nova Scotia coast 59 hours later after an almost trouble-free crossing, and went on to arrive over New York on 6th July. On the return trip she was diverted to Pulham after a journey from New York lasting 75 hours. Thus the R34 had become the first airship in history to cross the Atlantic, and the first airship to complete the double crossing.

In October that same year, the decision was taken to close East Fortune. It was too small; there were navigational difficulties — notably fog, and the hazard of North Berwick Law. East Fortune was to have a later and different contribution to make to the life of humanity.

The task facing North Berwick after the war was how to adapt to the new situation. Times had changed. The higher cost of living, increasing Income Tax and Death Duties meant that some establishments of the Edwardian era in North Berwick, the summer houses of the well-to-do, had to be either scaled down or sold. Some servants were pensioned off, many of them being generously treated by their former employers, and their future secured. The division of large houses into flats had not yet become the norm. Many large houses remained in the possession of their owners, as before, the Esmonds (related to the Rothschilds) in Marly Knowe, for example, and the Tennants (the family from whom Baroness Elliot is sprung) in Glenconner, as well as the traditional landed proprietors, the Duke of Hamilton, and others.

Under its Provost and the Town Clerk A. D. Wallace, the Town Council worked to preserve the image of North Berwick in the post-war world. All the town's exterior metalwork — lampposts, railings, bollards, and the rest — were painted silver. Great care was taken to keep the town's streets spotless, and the beach clean. The swimming pool must have a superintendent and instructors of quality: so, each summer, physical education teachers from Edinburgh schools were appointed to these posts. The proprietors of the pleasure launches took great pride in keeping their craft fresh and brightly painted.

It was with some justification that a later Provost of North Berwick, George Gilbert, would often incorporate in his public utterances his version of a quotation from the Book of Psalms — "Our lines are fallen in pleasant places".

Golf, of course, was still the big attraction. North Berwick continued to cater for golfers and for family holidaymakers to the best of its ability. The Marine Hotel still sent its ageing mini-bus to the railway station to collect clients. House-letting to summer visitors by the average house-owner in North Berwick continued strongly, and two of the main grocers in the town, M. and A. Edington and George Sheil and Son, compiled registers of lettings and visitors. One further factor in the popularisation of North Berwick for family holidays was the start of the bus service from Edinburgh, which was well patronised, although the journey took longer by bus than by train, and was not so comfortable. Increasing numbers of private cars also brought holidaymakers to the town.

Apart from golf, there were now a number of other attractions for visitors. The swimming pool has already been mentioned. There were the pleasure launches *St Baldred* and *St Nicholas,* later to be joined by the *Britannia,* and there were rowing boats for hire. George Fowler had open charabancs painted dark green and polished to a mirror finish, which would take visitors on tours round the places of interest in East

One of George Fowler's charabancs of the 1920's

"The Pierrots" — *Joe Anderson's Entertainers, 1924. Joe Anderson is second from the right*

Lothian: and there were the entertainers ("the Pierrots") at the open-air stage on the esplanade, afternoon and evening, under the leadership first, of Fred Erick, then of Joe Anderson. By the early 1930's the Foresters' Hall had become the Playhouse cinema. There were putting courses, two on the west and two on the east links, and there were tennis courts and a bowling green. For use during hard frosty weather there was a curling pond near the foot of Trainer's Brae, though this would be of use to residents in the town rather than visitors.

North Berwick might do much to attract visitors, for that had become its bread and butter, but the native population presented a different problem. The inter-war years saw the continuation of rural depopulation, which affected North Berwick. It also saw the General Strike of 1926 and the depression of the early '30's. Hotels and boarding houses, even at their best, afforded only seasonal employment, and with changing economic conditions they might be there one year and gone the next. To pushing penniless young men anxious to earn a good living, North Berwick had little to offer. To some, however, golf provided the magic key. Given skill and confidence at that game, much might be achieved.

Wilfred Thomson went to the United States in 1921 and stayed until 1937, when he returned to North Berwick. During his stay in America, he was professional, successively, at Country Club, Richmond, Virginia; Burning Tree in Washington; Hermitage in Richmond; and Holston Hills, Knoxville.

His son, Jimmy Thomson, went to America when he was 14. He became one of the leading professionals in the 1930's, and lived to become, in his time, the world's longest hitter. He won the North American Driving Championship held on the Canadian side of Niagara Falls, in 1937. To quote his own reported words "Everybody hit 20 drives. They averaged the ten best. My average was 316 yards and my best 386." An American journalist said of him "He was to golf what Babe Ruth was to baseball". He himself is reported as saying "My father was a great believer in balance. He believed the quieter you stand and the faster you use your hands, the better you'll hit . . . when I was 13 or 14 years old I began with a 9 iron and stood very quiet with my feet together. I was able to work up enough hand speed to get normal distances with the club. When I was 16 or 17 I got so I could hit a drive 225 yards with my feet together. . . . I always used light clubs. I used 13 ounces and lighter drivers all my life. . . . I believe to this day you can hit the ball better with lighter clubs. You get faster hand action that way."

At East Fortune, the buildings formerly used by airmen became a sanatorium for the treatment of tuberculosis in its many forms in 1922, under Dr Charles Cameron, who was later appointed Professor of Tuberculosis at Edinburgh University, and his assistant, Dr William A. Murray. In this capacity, East Fortune served the community until after the outbreak of the Second World War when the R.A.F. took it over as an operational airfield: and the sanatorium was moved to Bangour, West Lothian. During the inter-war years, much good work was done at East Fortune. Surgery of tubercular bones, joints, glands and kidneys, as well as thoracoplasty for pulmonary tuberculosis was undertaken successfully. In this work the distinguished surgeon Sir Walter Mercer played an important part. It must be appreciated that in this period neither anti-tubercular drugs nor the substances which made deep surgery possible had yet been developed. This had to wait till after the war.

A second line of attack against tuberculosis was, however, being deployed at Fenton Barns during the 1920's with the development of tuberculin tested herds of cows, giving a quantity output of milk free from the danger of causing bovine tuberculosis. This "T.T" milk was widely used. It supplied all the milk needs of the East Fortune sanatorium, and set a standard which became the norm for all milk production in days to come. This work was carried on by Dr Douglas Chalmers-Watson who, before starting the Fenton Barns project in 1923, had been a medical practitioner in Edinburgh.

Meantime, in the town of North Berwick, the social cachet of familiarity with the great was still strong, as illustrated by a story which has been handed down from the early 1920's. The scene is St Baldred's Episcopal Church. It is a summer Sunday morning. The church is full of society figures. The service is about to begin. Enter Lady Asquith, widow of Lord Asquith, former Liberal Prime Minister, to her seat, along with her household. Enter also Canon Marriot, along with a pale young curate (later to become Canon Gooderham). At this, Lady Asquith snaps her fingers, summoning the verger. The verger comes as rapidly as his dignity will allow. "Ask Canon Marriot,"

The area where the housing estate now stands

"The Gunboat" — a tenement in Forth Street, now demolished

says Lady Asquith, "if *that young man* (indicating the curate) is to be preaching to us today." The verger delivers his message to Canon Marriot and returns. "Canon Marriot," he says, "asks you, ma'am, if you will kindly follow the advice of your distinguished husband and Wait and See."

For the fishing community, the 1920's were years of change. There was a serious decline in line fishing. Seine-netting by trawlers was destroying the breeding stock of fish, and making the line-fisher's work unprofitable. By the early '30's the traditional scene of women baiting the lines with mussels at the harbour was vanishing. The traditional houses of these families were vanishing also. On the south side of Forth Street, just to the west of the Auld Hoose stood a property known as The Gunboat, which accommodated many families and which was demolished at this time. Simultaneously, the Town Council's housing scheme was taking shape, providing new and more modern accommodation, occupying the space between Dunbar Road and Law Road, near the foot of the Law.

North Berwick's industry in the 1920's consisted mainly in Ben Sayers' manufacture of golf clubs and Macintyre's aerated water factory. Ben Sayers' premises were those now occupied by D. S. Crawford's baker's shop, with the workshop at the back, in Forth Street where, until well into the 1950's, the mechanical hammer would strike out its note on the anvil as club after club was forged.

Among the young people of North Berwick in the post-First-World-War period are to be found two who are sons of the manse and who themselves became noted churchman of their time. These are the Revs. Robert Leonard Small and Nevile Davidson. The former is a son of the Rev. Robert Small, minister of Abbey Church, who, after a distinguished record as a student in Arts and Divinity at Edinburgh University, Rome, Berlin and Zürich, became minister successively of St John's, Bathgate; West High Church, Kilmarnock; Cramond; and St Cuthbert's Parish Church, Edinburgh. In North Berwick his contemporaries recall that he was dux of North Berwick High School, Scoutmaster, and member of the Bass Rock Football Club. As a keen footballer, he played as an amateur for St Bernard's F.C. in 1928-29 and was "capped" against England in 1929. He was made a Doctor of Divinity in 1957.

Nevile Davidson was the son of the Rev. James Davidson,

minister of Blackadder Church. He had a distinguished student career at Edinburgh University, becoming assistant lecturer in the Department of Mental Philosophy at that University, for a short time. His ministerial career began in 1925 at St Mary's Church, Aberdeen. Then, from 1932 to 1935 he was minister of St Enoch's, Dundee. The main phase of his career began in 1935 when he was appointed minister of Glasgow Cathedral, where he remained until his retirement in 1967. During his ministry there, the ancient building was enriched with many new stained glass windows. In the 1960's he gained the St Mungo Prize, given to the man who had done most for the city of Glasgow. He was for a time Chaplain in the King's Own Scottish Borderers. He was given the degree of Doctor of Divinity by Glasgow University in 1943 and was appointed Chaplain to King George VI in 1946.

Local tradition, however, preserves another facet of Dr Davidson's character. North Berwick people who remember him recall how in his boyhood he was full of high-spirited pranks; how on his bicycle he would tear down Law Road at full speed and then turn hard right into Kirk Ports to the danger of everyone's life and limb; and how he would cycle along the high and narrow parapet of the wall along the east bay sea front. For these and other escapades in his youth he earned himself the affectionately-given nickname Nevile the Devil.

Both of these ministers were appointed Moderators, in their turn, of the General Assembly of the Church of Scotland, and both were appointed Queen's Chaplains.

Until the outbreak of war in 1939, North Berwick continued to cater, as it had done, for golfers and for family holidaymakers. Ben Sayers' clubs had worldwide sale. Small yachts and dinghies were seen in the harbour in increasing numbers. Despite the decline in line-fishing, fishing for crab and lobster continued to be profitable.

In regard to the churches, the Act of Union of 1929 which made Abbey and Blackadder Churches into sister parish churches with St Andrew's, did not have the immediate effect of bringing about unity of spirit among the three. The early '30's saw storm and tempest in their relations, one of the bones of contention being which church had the right to conduct a Sunday School in a small hall (now occupied by the Royal British Legion) in Dunbar Road, for the benefit of children of people living in the Town Council's housing scheme nearby. Happily, this issue is now purely historic, and the weather pattern of relations may be described as "set fair" between the churches.

During the Second World War, public access to the east coast was restricted, but life went on in the little community, now numbering just over 4,000 souls. St Andrew's Parish Church Hall once again became a canteen for the forces. North Berwick, in short, shared the lot of wartime Britain. East Fortune again became an airfield, this time for the R.A.F.

It is at this point that we draw our history to a close — but North Berwick continues in the 1980's, facing the future in the knowledge that, so long as there are people who play golf, or people who like a seaside resort for their family holiday, its two golf courses, its two lovely sandy beaches, the interest of the Law, the islands of Fidra, the Lamb, Craigleith and the Bass, will together continue to attract those who wish to get away from city life for a holiday, or to retire from it fully, and spend the rest of their days among the kindly people of the town, so that their lines, too, may "fall in pleasant places".

I

SOURCES AND AUTHORITIES

Earliest Times

Who are the Scots? — ed. Gordon Menzies (BBC, 1971).

James B. Johnston — Place names in Scotland (3rd edition, John Murray, London, 1934).

The *Aberdeen Breviary,* Vol. 1, folio 64.

Symeon of Durham, ed. Arnold — (1) History of the Church of Durham, bk. 2, ch. 2. (2) History of St Cuthbert, ch. 4. (3) History of the Kings, ch. 84.

Rev. David C. MacFarlane and Kirk Session of Aberlady — Guide to the Parish Church of Aberlady, 1967.

Rev. Sidney Adamson — St Michael's Church at Inveresk.

The Venerable Bede — Historia Ecclesiastica Gentis Anglorum (ed. Moberley, Clarendon Press, Oxford, 1849).

Chronicles of Florence of Worcester (ed. Joseph Stevenson), s.a. 721.

Chronicle of Melrose (ed. Joseph Stevenson), s.a. 756/7.

Chronicles of the Picts and Scots.

A. O. Curle — The Treasure of Traprain.

Article on "The sources of the Life of St Kentigern" in "Studies in the Early British Church" — K. H. Jackson and others (Cambridge University Press, 1958).

J. M. Mackinlay — Ancient Church Dedications in Scotland, Vol. 2, pp 18-20.

Eddius Stephanus — Life of Wilfrid (in "Lives of the Saints" — Penguin Classics).

The Middle Ages

Turgot — Life of Saint Margaret — ed. Forbes-Leith, Edinburgh, 1896.

Article on the North Berwick Ferry by George Law in Scottish Historical Review, Vol. 2, 1905.

Carte Monialium de Northberwic — ed. Cosmo Innes (Bannatyne Club, 1847).

A. O. Anderson — Early Sources of Scottish History, Vol. 2, p. 523.

"Bagimond's Roll" — Scottish Historical Society's Miscellany, Vol. 6, p. 75.

Joseph Whitaker — article on Dovecotes in Transactions of the East Lothian Antiquarian and Field Naturalists Society, Vol. 3, 1938.

W. Cunningham — Growth of English Industry and Commerce (Cambridge University Press 1905) — see Appendix, in which is quoted Francesco Balducci Pegolotti — "La Practica della Mercatura". This speaks of wool trade of certain Cistertian monasteries including Ghuldinghamo (Coldingham) and Norbonucche (North Berwick).

Geoffrey Chaucer — Prologue to the Canterbury Tales (ed. A. W. Pollard, Macmillan, 1929).

NORTH BERWICK in the later Middle Ages

The "Ragman Roll".

Henry the Minstrel — (Blind Harry) — The Actis and deidis of the illustre and vailzeand campioun Schir William Wallace, Bk. II.

In "Calendar of Entries in Papal Registers relative to Great Britain" — Papal letters, Vol. IV (1362-96), ed. Bliss and Twemlow, 1902. ref. s.a. 1384.

Petitions to the Pope, under the following dates — 1365, 1380 (three entries), 1389, 1406 (two entries).

Fasti Ecclesiae Scoticanae Medii Aevi (draft, 1959) (ref. John de Carrick).

Calendar of Documents relating to Scotland, s.a. 1312.

Scottish History Society — Wigtownshire Charters (ref. Alexander of N. Berwick).

Charter by King James VI (1568).

Jean Froissart — Chronicles of England, France and the adjoining countries . . . etc. (trans. Thos. Johnes 1805), Vol. VI, ch. 5. (Froissart's "Chronicles" is now available in paperback in the Penguin Classics series).

John Major (John Mayr) — Historia Majoris Britanniae (trans. Arch. Constable), Bk. 6, ch. 3 (ref. William of North Berwick).

The Laing Charters, s.a. 1435 (Charter of Robert Lawedar of Eddrintoun).

J. A. Duke — The Church of Scotland to the Reformation (Oliver & Boyd, 1937) (ref. John Mayr).

Thomas McCrie —The Life of John Knox, 2nd ed., 1813 (ref. John Mayr).

W. Forbes Gray and James H. Jamieson — East Lothian Biographies 1941, p. 95 (ref. John Mayr).

Lord Treasurer's Accounts, s.a. 1474.

Times of the Reformation

Carte Monialium de Northberwic — ed. Cosmo Innes (Bannatyne Club, 1847).

Accounts of the Masters of Works for building and repairing Royal Palaces and Castles, Vol. 1, 1529 — 1615, ed. Henry M. Paton, intro. lii and p. 71.

Register of the Great Seal of the Kings of Scots — many charters referring to lands in North Berwick in the sixteenth century.

Minutes of the Presbytery of Haddington, s.a. 1587 — re Manse and Glebe of North Berwick.

D. B. Swan — The Monastery of North Berwick.

T. M. Lindsay — History of the Reformation (T. & T. Clark, Edin., (1906) (general reference).

Calendar of State Papers relating to Scotland, Vol. 1, p. 120 and p. 136.

Register of the Privy Seal of the Kings of Scots, Vol. III, nos. 2486, 2612 and 2632.

Speak of the Devil

Godfrey Watson — Bothwell and the Witches (Robert Hale, London, 1975).

Sir James Melville — Memoirs.

"Newes from Scotland" (1591).

Register of the Privy Council, s.a. 1613.

The Seventeenth Century

The Session Books of the Kirk of North Berwick, 1604-1616 and 1661-1685.

Register of the Privy Council, s.a. 1607 and 1689.

John Taylor — The penniless pilgrimage . . . etc, as quoted in text (1618).

Minutes of the Presbytery of Haddington, under dates quoted.

Hector Macpherson — Outlaws for freedom (Protestant Institute of Scotland, 1956).

John M. Duncan — The Parochial Ecclesiastical Law of Scotland — revised by C. N. Johnston Bell & Bradfute, Edin., 1903.

R. P. Phillimore — The Bass Rock.

Article on "Lists of Schoolmasters teaching Latin" — ed. Donald J. Withrington (Scottish History Society's Miscellany).

Article on "Timothy Pont map of the Tyne valley" in Transactions of the East Lothian Antiquarian and Field Naturalists Society, Vol. 7, p. 44.

References in writings of D. B. Swan to now lost Kirk Session Minutes of the 1650's.

The Eighteenth Century — and later

Turnbull's Diary (Minister of Tyninghame) in Scottish History Society's Miscellany, Vol. 1, p. 409.

Reports from the Scotch Education Department to the Rev. G. W. Sprott, D.D.

The Autobiography of Dr Alexander Carlyle of Inveresk — ed. J. Hill Burton (T. N. Foulis, Edinburgh, 1910).

Notes on the Dalrymple family kindly extracted from family papers by Sir Hew Hamilton-Dalrymple.

Notes on the Grant-Suttie family kindly supplied by Miss Hilda Grant-Suttie.

"Gentleman's Magazine", April 1746.

Bishop Pococke — Tour through Scotland, 1760.

Information on Robert and William Anderson kindly supplied by Miss Averil Lysaght.

Alexander Haldane — Memoirs of the Lives of Robert Haldane of Airthrey and of his brother James Alexander Haldane (Hamilton Adams & Co., London, and W. Whyte & Co., Edinburgh, 1852).

Sinclair — First Statistical Account of Scotland.

List of heads of families . . . etc., as quoted in text.
Minutes of North Berwick Town Council.

"The Biarritz of the North"

John Thomas — Regional History of the Railways of Great
Britain, Vol. 6, pp. 91-2.

Newspaper reports from the *Scotsman* and *Haddingtonshire
Courier".*

Personal reminiscences of Miss Diana Anderson, daughter of the
Rev. F. L. M. Anderson.

Rev. E. S. P. Heavenor — Abbey Milestones (Tantallon Press,
1963).

Our Lady Star of the Sea 1879-1979 (Centenary booklet)
(Tantallon Press, 1979).

Fasti Ecclesiae Scoticanae.

Written reminiscences of George Sayers, in an American golf
newsletter.

Personal reminiscences of various members of the Sayers family.

The collected papers of D. B. Swan, former Registrar of North
Berwick.

Personal reminiscences of Mr Alexr. Strachan.

Ian Brodie — Steamers of the Forth (David & Charles, Newton
Abbot, 1976).

Recent times 1914-1939

Published material on East Fortune as R.N.A.S. station.

American newspaper cuttings re Jimmy Thomson, by courtesy of
Mrs Catherine Pearson.

Personal reminiscences of Dr William Murray, re East Fortune
Sanatorium.

Rupert G. Chalmers-Watson, O.B.E. — Fenton Barns and
associate farms 1923-73

Fasti Ecclesiae Scoticanae.

Where use has been made of information contained in any of
the above publications, the author freely acknowledges these as
his source.

ACKNOWLEDGMENTS

SUCH A BOOK as this cannot be written without incurring a debt of gratitude to a large number of people and public bodies, for a great variety of "services rendered".

First, I am grateful to the Community Council of North Berwick, for their unfailing interest and their zeal for the project; and especially to Chairman Lyle Crawford and Councillors Ben Millar and Ruth Tweedie, for all the help they gave both as members of the Council and as personal friends. Then, my very grateful thanks goes to Sir Hew Hamilton-Dalrymple for not only writing the preface but supplying most valuable information on the part members of his family have played in the affairs of North Berwick of old.

I acknowledge also the help of East Lothian District Council, and the courtesy of the North Berwick Museum Management Committee in making available exhibits in the Museum for purposes of illustration. I thank the Kirk Session of the Parish Church of St Andrew, North Berwick, for placing its historical material at my disposal, and I also thank Mr C. J. S. Addison, one of its members, for his help in connection with some of the ecclesiastical investigations. I thank the Royal Commission on the Ancient and Historical Monuments of Scotland for permission to reproduce the photograph of North Berwick Railway Station in the 1920's, and I thank Aerofilms Ltd. for the aerial view of North Berwick reproduced on the dust jacket. Other illustrations were derived from the collection belonging to the North Berwick Environment Trust, and to them also I am grateful. For yet other illustrations, I have been permitted to use photographs and paintings in private hands, and so my thanks are due to Mr William Auld, Mrs Nanny Crawford, Mr A. F. Hodgson, Mr David Millar, Miss Annie Mackay, Mrs B. Tait, Miss Madge Wallace, Mr Robert Walton, and the doctors of the North Berwick Group Medical Practice, for their courtesy and assistance. I am indebted also to Mr K. S. Bell for his help and advice in regard to setting out the contents of this book.

Finally, I am especially grateful to my wife and family. Without their patience and their understanding over an extended period, the work on this book could not have been carried out.

INDEX

Abbey Church, 69, 70

Abbey farm buildings, 16, 25

Abbey of North Berwick — see Nunnery of North Berwick

Abbey Old People's Home, 15

Abeloc, Thomas, 22

Aberdeen, 42, 43, 45
St Mary's Church, 86

Aberdeen Breviary, 4, 8, 9

Aberdeen, Canon of (William of North Berwick), 28

Aberlady, 2, 6, 8, 68

Aberlady, Gullane and North Berwick Railway Co., 68

Aberlessic, 2, 10

Abuses in the Church, 27

Acca, bishop of Hexham, 9

"Acmootye, Master John", 46

Adam brothers, 64

Adamson, John, parish minister of North Berwick, 44

Aebba, princess and abbess, 5

Aethelwald, abbot, later bishop of Lindisfarne, 8

Aidan, monk of Iona, 5

Ainslie, Walter, schoolmaster in North Berwick, 54

Albert Edward, Prince of Wales, afterwards King Edward VII, 67

Alexander III, King of Scots, 23

Alexander, vicar of North Berwick, 25

Alexandra, Queen, 72

Alloway, old kirk of, 42

Anderson, F. L. M., Episcopal Rector of North Berwick, 69

Anderson, Joe, leader of entertainers, 83

Anderson, Robert, schoolmaster in North Berwick, 62

Anderson, Sir Rowand, architect, 71

Anderson, William, surgeon and naturalist, 62

Andrew, Saint, 5, 9, 14
parish church of — see Parish Church of St Andrew

Angus, Earl of, 31

Anlaf the Dane, 10

Anne, princess of Denmark, 39

Anti-Popes, 27

Antonine Wall, 1

Arbroath, 36

Archerfield, 69

Asquith, Lady, 84

Asquith, Lord, Prime Minister, 84

Assembly, General, of the Church of Scotland, 45, 86

Associate Synod, 70

Atlantic Ocean, 81

Auchindore, in diocese of Aberdeen, 28

Auld, William, and Son, 70

Augustine, Saint, of Canterbury, 5

Auldhame, 4, 8, 11, 46

Auld Hoose, 85

Avignon, 27, 29

Babe Ruth, 83

"Bagoon" — see Balgone

Baldred, Saint, 3-11, 34, 69

Baldred's Boat, 11

Balfour, Hon. A. J., Prime Minister, 77, 80

Balgone, 49, 51

Balliol, John, King of Scots, 23

Balmoral Castle, 76

Bangour, West Lothian, 84

Bannockburn, Battle of, 62

Barbe, Ste, College of, 31

Barndennoch, 52

Barony of North Berwick, 13, 37, 47, 55

Barre, Archibald, vicar of North Berwick, 34

Barton, Sir John, 32

Basilikon Doron, 42

Basle, 34

Bass Rock, 3, 6, 11, 31, 34, 46, 52, 54, 55, 64, 68, 87

Bass Rock Football Club, 85

Bass Rock Garage, 78

Bathgate: St John's Church, 85

Bathing regulations, 74

Beardmores, 81

Beaton, Cardinal David, 34

Beatrice, prioress, 17

Bede, the Venerable, monk of Jarrow, 5, 6, 8, 9

Bel, Walter, vicar of North Berwick, 26

Bell Rock, 36

Benedict XIII, Anti-Pope, 29

Benedictine Order, the, 15

Berlin, 85

Bernard's, Saint, Football Club, 85

Bernham, David de, bishop, 9, 16

Berry, Dr G. A., ophthalmic surgeon, 77

Berwick Law, 3

Berwick-upon-Tweed, 3, 13, 23, 62

Berwick, Sussex, 3

Blackadder Church, 53, 70, 86

Blackadder, John, Covenanter, 52, 53

"Black Death", the, 25

Blairhall, Fife, 52

Bonnington, 49

Bothwell, Earl of (Francis Stuart), 39-41

Bowling, Dunbartonshire, 1

Bowling at North Berwick, 76

Boys' Institute, 76

Braid, James, golfer, 73, 79

Brass Band, 76

Brechin, 42

British Red Cross Society, 77

Broad Sands, 14

Brodie, James, provost of North Berwick, 75

Broune, James, vicar of North Berwick, 34

Brown, —, surgeon in Haddington, 56

Bruce, Robert, King of Scots, 17, 23

Brythonic language, 2

Buchan, General, 54

Buchanan, George, 32

Bull, Stephen, commander of English naval force, 36

Burn, Capt. Robert, 63

Burning Tree Golf Club, Washington, U.S.A., 83

Burns, Robert, 3, 42

Burton-juxta-Beverley, 25

Bury, Lord, 60

Bus service, 82

Cadet Corps, 76

Cambridge University, 31

Corpus Christi College, 34

Cameron, Dr Charles, authority on tuberculosis, 84

Canteen for the Forces, 81

Carele (Crail) Fife, 28

Carlyle, Alexander, parish minister of Inveresk, 57

Carrick, Alexander, burgess of North Berwick, 36

Carrick, Elena de, prioress, 17, 29

Carrick, John de, Archdeacon of Sodor, 29

Castle Hill, 1

Chalmers-Watson, Dr Douglas, 84

Charlemagne, 12

Charles Edward, "the Young Pretender", 60

Chronicles of the Picts and Scots, 9

Church Service Society, 71, 74

Cistertian Order, the, 15

Clartie Burn, 20

Clifford Road, 21, 77

Coastguards, 76

Coastguard Cottages, 64

Cockburne, Mariot, prioress, 35

Coldingham, 6

Columba, Saint, 5

Congleton, 24

Connaught, Arthur, Duke of, 69, 72

Constance, Council of, 29

Corbridge, Thomas de, Archbishop of York, 25

Coronation mugs and medals, 76

Copenhagen, 39

Country Club, Richmond, Virginia, U.S.A., 83

Craigdarroch, Lady, 52

Craigleith, 12, 27, 46, 69, 87

Cramond: parish church, 85

Crawford, D. S. & Co., bakers, 85

Creich, Patrick, parish minister of North Berwick, 37

Crimean War, 77

Cromdale, 54

Cullen, 42

Culloden House, 60

Culross, 10

Cumberland, Duke of, 60

Cunningham, John, schoolmaster in "Saltpans in Lothian", 40

Curling pond, 83

Cuthbert, Saint, 4, 6

Dall, James, chief magistrate of North Berwick, 68

Dalrymple Arms Hotel, 50, 60

Dalrymple family, 59
  Sir John, Younger, of Stair (later Secretary of State), 53
  Hon. Sir Hew, Lord President of Court of Session, 55, 56
  Sir Hew, sixth baronet, 63, 68, 71
  Sir Walter, eighth baronet, 71, 75, 79
  Sir Hew Hamilton-Dalrymple (ninth baronet), 51
  Sir Hew Hamilton-Dalrymple (tenth baronet), 67

Dalrymple Garage, 25

Danes, 10

David II, King of Scots, 26

David, vicar of North Berwick, 22

Davidson, James, minister of Blackadder Church, 85
  Dr Nevile, minister of Glasgow Cathedral, 85

Demonologie, 42

Denmark, 39, 42, 43

Dere Street, 7

Deugaigne, John, valet de chambre, 15

"Devil" the, 39-43

Dick, Sir William, of Braid, burgess in Edinburgh, 47, 48
  Sir Andrew, 49

Dirleton, 14, 69

Dirleton Avenue, 16, 69, 75

Divine Right of Kings, 42

Domesday Book, 3

Douglas, Earls of, 13, 20, 55
  William, first earl, 13
  James, second earl, 28
  Gavin, 31

Drummer, Town, 63

Dumfries, 47, 52

Dunbar, 5, 42, 43

Duncan, Gilles, 40

Dundee: St Enoch's Church, 86

Dunpelder, 2

Eadbert, King of Northumbria, 4

Earlsferry, 13, 36

East Fortune, as airfield, 81, 84, 87
  as sanatorium, 84

East Lothian, 2, 3, 7, 8, 9, 10, 12, 34, 39, 45, 46, 58, 79, 82

Edinburgh, 34, 43, 44, 47, 52, 69, 79, 84
  Castle, 41
  Duke of, (afterwards, of Saxe-Coburg Gotha), 69

Edinburgh: St Cuthbert's Parish Church, 6, 85

Edington, M. and A., grocers, 82

Edward I, King of England, 23, 62

Edward II, King of England, 15, 25, 62

Edward VII, King, 68, 76, 77

Eggar, —, surgeon in Haddington, 56

Eil burn, 14

Elgin, 42

Elie, 78

Elizabeth I, Queen of England, 44

Elliot, Baroness, 82

Elsinore, 39

Entertainers, 77, 83

Episcopal Church in Scotland, 69

Erick, Fred, leader of entertainers, 83

Erskine, Ebenezer, 70

Escemuthe (Inveresk), 5, 6, 7

Esk, river, 6

Esmond family, 82

Estates of Scotland, 26, 35

Faber, Johannes, vicar of North Berwick, 26

Fennell, Arthur, golf professional, 73

Fenton Barns, 84

Fergus Ferguson, lifeboat, 78

96

Fermelandis, 35
Ferour, Schir Andrew, Chaplain of the Lady Altar, 30
Ferrygate, 14
"Fian, Doctor", 40, 41
Fidra, island, 3, 87
Fife, 9, 10
Fife, Earls of, 13, 15, 18
  Malcolm, 20
Fire Brigade, 76
Firefly, yacht, 68
Flamborough Head, 29
Florence of Worcester, chronicler, 8
Foresters' Hall, 75, 76, 79, 83
Forres, 42
Forth estuary, 13
Foster family, 64
Fowler, George, garage proprietor, 82
France, alliance of Scotland with, 23
Free Church, 53, 70
Freemasons, 76
French Ambassador, 61
French troops in East Lothian, 34
Friothubert, bishop of Hexham, 4
Froissart, Jean, chronicler, 28

Gaelic language, 12
Gas consumption, 78
Gasworks, 66, 77, 78
Geneva, influence of, 34, 37
Gibson, William, bishop, 34
Gilbert, George C., provost of North Berwick, 82
Gilbert, Michael, parish minister of North Berwick, 45
Gillecalmestun, 15
Gilsland, 77
Glasgow, Cathedral, 86
  John, Archbishop of, 45
Glass, James, Bailie of North Berwick, 76
Gleghornie, 31
Glen, James, parish minister of Dirleton, 58
Glover, T. S., schoolmaster in North Berwick, 75
Good Templars, 76
Goodale, Alexander, schoolmaster in North Berwick, 54

Gooderham, Canon, Rector of St Baldred's Episcopal Church, 84
Graham, Robert Balfour, parish minister of North Berwick, 64
  Henry Grey, historian, 64
Grant, Arthur, golf professional, 73
  Ben, golfer, 73
  David, golfer, 73
  Sir Francis, painter, 67
  Norman, golf professional, 73
Grant-Suttie family, 59
Grose, Capt. Francis, 42
Guild, Andrew, parish minister of North Berwick, 53
Guild, Lieut.-Col., 75
Guild of St Margaret, 71
Gullane, parish church of St Andrew, 9
"Gunboat", the, tenement building, 85
Gunpowder Plot, 44
Gutta-percha golf balls, 72

Haddington, Earl of, 77
Haddington, Grammar School of, 31
Hadrian's Wall, 1
Haldane, James, 62
Halfland Barns (Haflen Barns), 57
Hamilton, Ann (Lady Sydserf), 56
Hamilton, Duke of, 82
Hamilton, Patrick, 32, 34
Hamlet, 39
Hammermen, Edinburgh Guild of, 48
Harelaw, 49
Harvey, Dr William, 46
Heckilwelcros, 35
Henry VIII, King of England, 34
Henry the Minstrel (Blind Harry), 23, 24
Herbert, John, parish minister of North Berwick, 55
Herd, Sandy, golfer, 73
Hermitage Golf Club, Richmond, Va., U.S.A., 83
Hertford, Earl of, 34
Heugh, the, 49
Hexham, bishop of, 5, 8
High Street, 51, 60, 62, 67, 71, 75
Hill, Prof. Henry David, parish minister of North Berwick, *pro tem,* 58, 59
Himsworth, Thomas, bailie of North Berwick, 76

Historia Maioris Britanniae, 31
Holston Hills Golf Club, Knoxville, U.S.A., 83
Holyroodhouse, stone for ovens at, 33
Home, Alexander, "gudeman of North Berwick", 15, 35, 36, 44
   Andrew, 35
   Isabella, prioress, 35
   Sir John, baron, 44
   Margaret, prioress, 17, 35, 36
   Patrick, of Polwarth, 35
   Patrick, fifth baron, 47
Hospice for pilgrims, 13, 14
Hospital, infectious diseases, 77
House-letting, 82
Hugh, vicar of North Berwick, 21-22
Hutton, Col., 14, 60

Illumination of the town, 75, 77
Inchinnan, 81
Incuneningum, 8
Intiningaham, 8
Inveresk, 2, 6, 7
   parish church of St Michael, 7
Inverness, 42, 60

"J", vicar of North Berwick, 22
James I, King of Scots, 29
James III, King of Scots, 32
James V, King of Scots, 33, 39
James VI, King of Scots, later James I of the United Kingdom, 35, 39-42, 44
James, vicar of North Berwick, 29
Jedburgh, 7

Kay's Wynd (Law Road), 26
Kaye, James, golf professional, 72
Kelly family, 64
Kenneth MacAlpin, King of Scots, 12
Kent, Duchess of, mother of Queen Victoria, 69
Kentigern, Saint (Mungo), 4, 9
Kilconquhar, tiends of parish of, 36
   vicar of, 36
Kilmarnock, Earl of, 61
Kilmarnock: West High Church, 85
Kilmurdie, 12
Kinghorn, 23
King's Own Scottish Borderers, 86

Kinneil, 1
Kirkaldy, Andrew, golfer, 72, 73
Kirkcudbright, 6
   Thomas de, bishop of Candida Casa, 25
Kirknewton, "rectoria" of, 34
Kirk Ports, 52
Knoll, the, house name, 77
Knox, John, 32, 37
Knowis, George, burgess of Aberdeen, 42
Kronborg Castle, 39

Lamb, the, island, 87
Lammermuir, 7
Lamysyde (Lamside), 35
Largo, vicar of, 36
Lauder family, 25, 30, 37, 47
   burials, 30
   Robert, friend of Wallace, 24
   Sir Robert, of the Bass, 25
   Robert, notary in North Berwick, 25
   William, natural son of Robert Lauder of the Bass, 35
Lauder's hospital, 25, 60
Launches, pleasure, 82
Lawedar, Robert of, of Eddrintoun, knight, 30
Lawedre, Edward de, archdeacon of Lothian, 25
Law, the, 34, 56, 61, 63, 68, 85, 87
   horse race up, 73
   lookout posts on, 63
Law Road, 20, 21, 68
Leck, red, 33
Leith, 34, 72, 78
Leithies, the, 12
Leuchie, 55
Leys, Matilda de, prioress, 17
Library, National, of Scotland, 14
Lifeboat, 76, 78
Lifeboat Day, 78
Lindisfarne (Holy Island), 5
   diocese of, 4
   bishop of, 4, 8
Links, the, 35
Linlithgow, 73
   schoolmaster of, 34
Lockhart, W. E., R.S.A., painter, 51

Lollards, 27
Lombard, Peter, 31
Lombormore (Lammermuir), 5, 6, 7
Longniddry, 68
London, 15, 44, 69, 71, 80
  Tower of, 29
London and North Eastern Railway, 81
Loth, King, 10
Lothian, 7, 10, 12
  deanery of, 7
Louisa, H.M. gunboat, 68
Lyell, Sir George, curate of North
  Berwick, 36
Lyons, General Council at, 22

MacDonald, Archbishop (St Andrews
  and Edinburgh), 70
McGilchrist, James, gas engineer, 78
Macintyre, John, provost of North
  Berwick, 76, 77, 85
"Maid of Norway", the, 23
Mains farmhouse, 62
Malcolm III (Canmore), King of Scots,
  12
Margaret, Queen, 12, 13
Marine Hotel, 82
Marine Parade, 1
Marjoribanks family, 55
Market Cross, 26
Market Day, 26
Market Place, 62
Marly Knowe, 82
Marriot, Canon J., Rector of St
  Baldred's Church, 84
Mary Place, 65
May, Isle of, 9, 78
Mayr, John (John Major), 28, 31, 32
Melanchthon, Philip, 32
Melbourne Place, 60, 75
Melrose, Old, 6, 7, 8
Melville, James, professor, 15
Menzies, John, 48
Mercer, Sir Walter, surgeon, 84
Merion Club, Philadelphia, U.S.A., 72
Metalwork, exterior, painter silver, 82
Michael, Grand Duke, of Russia, 72
Middleton, Capt., 54
Mile, the Royal, 44
Millar family, 64

Milsey Bay, 17
Minto House, 69
Modwenna, Saint, 7
Monastery of North Berwick — see
  Nunnery of North Berwick
Montaigu, College of, 31
Monte Carlo, 73
Monteith, James, bellfounder in Edin-
  burgh, 48
Montrose, 42
Morham, 6, 8
Mungo, Saint (Kentigern), 4, 9, 10
Murray, George (1) parish minister of
  North Berwick, 57, 58
  George (2) parish minister of North
  Berwick, 58
  Matthew, parish minister of North
  Berwick, 58, 59
Murray, Mr —, of Broughton, 61
Murray, Dr W. A., 84

Nairn, 42
Newark, the, 35
Newcastle-upon-Tyne, 22
Newhouse, 12
Newstead (Trimontium), 7, 8
New York, 81
Niagara Falls, 83
North American Driving Championship,
  83
Northampton, Treaty of, 23
NORTH BERWICK, early Man in, 1
  ferry, 13-15
  Golf Club, 67
    "Corporation Golf Clubs", 79
  harbour, 14, 64, 66, 68
  Grammar School, 62
  High School, 85
  hospice, 13, 14, 20
  name of town, 2
  Royal Burgh of, i, 14, 26, 42, 43, 49,
    50, 58, 59, 62, 68, 75
  boundary of, 26
  coat of arms, 14, 76
  first charter of, 14, 26
  replacement charter of, 26
North Berwick, Maine, U.S.A., 3
North British Railway Co. Ltd., 68
Northumbria, 2, 5

Nova Scotia, 81
Nunnery of North Berwick (abbey, monastery, priory), 15-18, 29, 33, 37
  and agriculture, 16
  Church of St Mary, 16, 37
  date of, 15
  dovecote of, 16, 35
  endowments of, 18, 35, 36
  gardens and orchards of, 35
  manufacture of tiles at, 16
  Mills of Kintreath, 17, 35
  prioresses, 17, 18, 24, 35, 36
    "James, Prior of North Berwick", 15
  site of, 15
  wool from, 17

Oddfellows, 76
Olaf Godfreyson, 10
Olilaf, 5, 10
Oldfields, house name, 16
Open Championship, British (golf), 72, 79
Ordination, Sacrament of, 21
Otadeni — see Votadini
Our Lady, Star of the Sea, Church of, 70
Oxford University, 31
Oxford, Bishop of, 69

Paris, University of, 31
Parish Church of St Andrew
  (1) at harbour, 9, 18, 61, 66, 76
    altars, 19, 20, 30, 37
    bell, 19, 48
    construction, 18, 19, 59, 60
    date, 18, 20
    destruction by storm, 19, 42, 49
    glebe, 21, 37, 73
    grave stones, 19
    Manse (vicarage house), 20, 37
    mould for pilgrims' badges, 14
    tower, 19
    vicars, 20-22, 23, 25, 26, 29, 34, 36, 37
  (2) in Kirk Ports, 50-51, 70
    choice of site, 50, 51
    construction, 51
    date, 51
    proposed extension of, 71
    graveyard, 51, 53
    sundial, 51

  (3) in High Street, 20, 21, 71, 75
    date, 71
    design, 71
    Hall, 71, 81, 87
    Tower, 71
    memorial window to Queen Victoria, 76
    Manse, 64
Parliaments, Union of the, 56
Peffer (name of stream), 2
Perth, Council at, 22
Piccolomini, Aeneas Silvius, Papal Legate, 30
Picts, 9, 12
Pier, Galloway's, 79
"Pierrots", the — see Entertainers
Pilgrims, 13-15
Pipe Band, 76
Pitcarn, —, younger, physician in Haddington, 56
Pius, II, Pope, 31
Playhouse Cinema, 83
Pococke, Bishop, 61
Point Garry Hotel, 78
Pont, Timothy, cartographer, 45
Pope, 12, 33, 34, 37
  authority of, 12, 33, 34, 37
Poor, relief of the, 48
Postmaster, 67
Preston (= Prestonkirk), 3, 4, 8, 11
Prestonpans, 39, 40, 60
Pretoria, 75
Priesthood of all believers, 50
Primmer, Jacob, minister in Dunfermline, and pamphleteer, 74
Priory of North Berwick — see Nunnery of North Berwick
Privy Council, 42, 43, 44, 53, 54
Pulham, 81

Quadrant, 69, 75
Quality Street (Trongate), 50, 59, 60, 67, 68
Queensferry, 13

R34, airship, 81
Rabelais, François, satirist, 32
"Ragman Roll", 23
Railway Station, 66, 76, 82
Redgauntlet, pleasure steamer, 79

Reformation, 4, 11, 15, 32-37, 50
Reformed churches in France, 47
Reid, Matthew, parish minister of North Berwick, 55-59
Relief Synod, 70
Richard, Chaplain, 20
Richardson, James S., LL.D., i, 8, 14, 19, 25, 35, 61, 66
Richartsoun, Thom, landholder in North Berwick, 30
Robert II, King of Scots, 13, 14, 26
Robert III, King of Scots, 29
Rochelle, La, 47
Rocket Brigade, 76
Roman times, 1
Rome, Bishop of, 12
Rosehill (house name), 21
Rothschild family, 82
Royal Air Force, 84
Royal British Legion, 86
Royal Hotel, 66
Royal Naval Air Service, 81
Royal Scots, 81

St Andrew Street, 21
St Andrews, Fife, 9, 13, 14, 32, 37
St Andrews, Bishop of, 29
St Andrews, Archbishop of, 11, 25, 33, 34, 45
St Andrews, University of, 15, 32
  St Salvator's College, 32
"St Mungo Prize", 86
Sampson, Agnes, 41
Sandby, Paul, painter, 59
Sandwich, 79
Saxe-Weimar, Edward, Prince of, 72, 77
Sayers, Ben, golf professional, 72, 73, 79, 85
  George, golf professional, 72
Scots, 12
"Scotsman", the, newspaper, 67, 68, 75
Scoutmaster, 85
Seaton Carew, 72
Sebastian, Saint, 20, 25
Serf (Servanus), Saint, 10
Shakespeare, William, 39
Shiel, George, and Son, grocers, 82

Sinclare, Patrick, vicar of North Berwick, 34
  William, vicar of North Berwick, 34
Slaughterhouse, 77
Small, Dr R. Leonard, 85
Soutra, 7
Sowhole, 65
Sowty, Sir George — see Suttie, Sir George
Speed, John, cartographer, 45
Speir family, 15
Spittal, Longniddry, 68
Sprott, G. W., D.D., parish minister of North Berwick, 57, 71, 74, 75
Stalpart, Cristiane, landholder in North Berwick, 30
Station Hill, 66
Steamers, Galloway, 78
Stephanus, Eddius, biographer of Wilfrid, 5
Stevenson, Robert Louis, author, 69
Stewart, —, physician in Haddington, 56
Strain, Archbishop, 70
Strathallan, Lord, 61
Struth, Alexr., 73
Stuart dynasty, 17, 42
Stuart, Francis, Earl of Bothwell, 39-41
Sunday School, 86
Sunningdale, 79
Superstitions, 38
Suttie family, 51, 59
Suttie, Sir George, of Balgone, 59
Swimming Pool, 77, 82
Sydserf, Lady (Ann Hamilton), 56
Symeon, monk of Durham, 3-10

Taft, President, 73
Tain, 42
Tam o' Shanter, 42
Tantallon (name), 2
Tantallon Castle, 13, 31, 55, 62, 69
Tantallon Castle, pleasure steamer, 79
Taylor, J. H., golfer, 73
Taylor, John, "water-poet", 46
Tennant family, 82
Thenew, princess, 10

101

Thomson, Jimmy, golf professional, 79, 83

Thomson, Wilfred, golf professional, 79, 83

Tiends, 18

Tiningaham — see Tyninghame

Tompson, Agnes, 41

Train service, 74, 75

Trainer's Brae, 83

Traprain Law, 2, 10

Traprain, Treasure of, 10

Timontium (Newstead), 7

Trongate (Quality Street), 59, 60

Tuberculin tested milk, 84

Tuberculosis, 84

Turgot, biographer of Margaret, Saint and Queen, 12

Turnbull, George, parish minister of Tyninghame, 56

Tweed, river, 6

Tyne (East Lothian) river, 10, 31

Tyninghame, 4, 5, 6, 8, 10, 11, 46

Tyninghame, Dean of, 10

Tyninghame House, 77

Tyninghame, Lord, 11

Umpire, horse, 73

United Associate Congregation, 70

United Free Church of Scotland, 70

United Presbyterian Church of Scotland, 69, 70

United Secession Church, 70

Vardon, Harry, golfer, 73

Vennel, the common, 30

Vicars of North Berwick — see under Parish Church of St Andrew

Vici, Baiamundo de, Canon of Asti, 22

Victoria, Queen, 64, 75
  diamond jubilee of, 75

Victoria House, 62

Volunteer Artillery Corps, 63

Volunteers, the, North Berwick, 63, 75, 76

Votadini (Otadeni), 1, 2

Waldeve, vicar of North Berwick, 21, 23

Wall Tower, 9, 59

Wallace, A. D., Town Clerk, 82

Wallace, Capt. John, 16

Wallace, Sir William, 23, 24

War of Independence, 23, 24

Waterloo, battle of, 64

Water Supply, 77

Wedderburn, Sir John, 61

Westgate, 20, 70

Whitby, Synod of, 5

White, Jack, golf professional, 73, 79

Whitekirk, parish church of (St Mary), 31, 34

Whitelaw, Mrs J. B., 81

Whitelaw, Sir William, 81

Wilfrid, bishop of Hexham, 5, 9

William, bishop of Aberdeen, 36

William, vicar of North Berwick, 25

William of North Berwick (alias de Lundie), vicar of North Berwick, 27, 28, 29

Williamston, 78

Wishart, George, 34

Witchcraft, 38-42

Woman's Guild of the Church of Scotland, 71

Wonderland (former house name), 21

Wood (or Wod) Alexander, vicar of North Berwick, 36

Wood (or Wod) Sir Andrew, of Largo, 36

Wod, Alison, natural daughter of Alexr. Wod, vicar of North Berwick, 36

  Jonet, natural daughter of Alexr. Wod, vicar of North Berwick, 36

  Robert, natural son of Alexr. Wod, vicar of North Berwick, 36

Wyclif, John, 27

Yachting at North Berwick, 86

Yeomanry, 76

Yester, 2

York, Archbishop of, 25

York Road, 69, 75

Young, John, parish minister of North Berwick, 37

Zeppelins, 80

Zürich, 34, 35